Persian Blues, Psychoanalysis and Mourning

In *Persian Blues, Psychoanalysis and Mourning*, Gohar Homayounpour plays a theme and variations on loss, love, and family against the backdrop of Iran's chaotic recent past.

Homayounpour is simultaneously Shahrzad, the fearless storyteller, and Shahrzad's analyst: subjecting fairy tales to fierce new insights, while weaving an indigo thread through her own devastation on the death of her father and the wonders and horrors of motherhood. A blue thread, or melody, runs though the separations and emigrations of her family and patients driven or broken apart by war, and likewise through the fraught world inhabited by Persian women. This book breaks new psychoanalytic ground, offering a radical rejection of traditional clichés about Iran, and Iranian women, but its unsparing elegance transcends any political agenda, bridging the ocean of a shared and tragic humanity.

Persian Blues, Psychoanalysis and Mourning will be of great interest to psychoanalysts and psychoanalytically informed readers, as well as those interested in grief, Iran, and women's experiences.

Gohar Homayounpour is a psychoanalyst and Gradiva award-winning author. She is a member of the International Psychoanalytic Association and the American Psychoanalytic Association, a training and supervising psychoanalyst of the Freudian Group of Tehran, and a scientific board member of the Sigmund Freud Museum in Vienna.

"*Persian Blues* will be known as one of the great experimental and poetic discourses on the subversive character of psychoanalysis in our times. A practicing analyst in Tehran, but also a writer and theorist, Homayounpour poses the question of what one may expect from psychoanalysis. The answers she gives are drawn from the world of dreams, sessions, screen-memories, poems, stories, and theories, as well as reports on historical and political events to make the answer at once enigmatic and urgent.

A brilliant foray into both memory and imagination, eclectic and pointed, this work underscores the ethics that psychoanalysis yields, the difficult work of mourning within the time of one's life, and the historical and geopolitical realities and cultural debates within which psychoanalysis must renew itself. Navigating debates on the veil, Eurocentrism, and super-egoic discourses of the everyday, Homayounpour proves to be a shrewd cultural critic of our times.

In the face of devastating losses, Homayounpour cautions against the wish to have all our wounds healed. She insists that life is lived well not in spite of our wounds, but because of them. Indeed, the ethical potential yielded by a curtailed narcissism is found in the distance, the difference, between self and other, need and object – vital disjunctures within relations of love. This text not only reads across theoretical, clinical, and poetic genres to interrogate love and ambivalence, but is itself a loving text, a gift of love; that is, a petition to encounter the difficulty that makes us into subjects who can love."

Judith Butler

"Gohar Homayounpour's new book takes us on a musical, unpredictable, and lively journey, through psychoanalysis, autobiography, social commentary, and culture. Avoiding the usual formats of both analytic prose and memoir, she forges a unique and deeply personal text which will appeal not only to analysts and students of psychoanalysis, but to a much wider readership."

Darian Leader, *psychoanalyst and member of the Centre for Freudian Analysis and Research, UK*

"Dr Gohar Homayounpour, an Iranian psychoanalyst who started the Freudian Group of Tehran, has written a brilliant meditation on a psychoanalyst's life. The book is an integration of personal, cultural, philosophical, political, and clinical ideas, always within the context of a deeply reflective psychoanalytic mind. In *Persian Blues* you will meet a unique psychoanalyst and be glad for the experience."

Fred Busch, *member of the International Psychoanalytic Association and the American Psychoanalytic Association, USA*

"The equation is a simple one: Gohar Homayounpour's *Persian Blues* is to psychoanalysis what Bob Dylan's lyrics and music are to Mozart's Symphony No. 41. Persian Blues *essentially shows that psychoanalysis was, is, and will be the gay science of subjectivity.* I envy the reader who can discover the exceptional beauty of psychoanalysis as an interweaving of the teachings of their great ancestors, history lived through personal experience, erudition, and the sublimity of the very best of music and poetry played on the stage of the dreamer."

Néstor Braunstein, *Professor, Universidad Nacional Autónoma de México, Doctor Honoris Causa, Universidad Veracruzana, Mexico*

Persian Blues, Psychoanalysis and Mourning

Gohar Homayounpour

R Routledge
Taylor & Francis Group

LONDON AND NEW YORK

Cover image: "Lakes Drying, Tides Rising, 2021" (detail) by Nazgol Ansarinia

First published 2023
by Routledge
4 Park Square, Milton Park, Abingdon, Oxon OX14 4RN

and by Routledge
605 Third Avenue, New York, NY 10158

Routledge is an imprint of the Taylor & Francis Group, an informa business

British Library Cataloguing-in-Publication Data
A catalogue record for this book is available from the British Library

Library of Congress Cataloging-in-Publication Data
Names: Homayounpour, Gohar, 1977- author.
Title: Persian blues, psychoanalysis and mourning / Gohar Homayounpour.
Description: Milton Park, Abingdon, Oxon ; New York, NY : Routledge, 2023. |
Includes bibliographical references and index. |
Identifiers: LCCN 2022005260 (print) | LCCN 2022005261 (ebook) |
ISBN 9781032208053 (hardback) | ISBN 9781032215945 (paperback) |
ISBN 9781003269113 (ebook)
Subjects: LCSH: Bereavement--Iran--Psychological aspects. | Women--Iran. |
Psychoanalysis--Iran.
Classification: LCC BF575.G7 H6557 2023 (print) | LCC BF575.G7 (ebook) |
DDC 155.9/3--dc23/eng/20220207
LC record available at https://lccn.loc.gov/2022005260
LC ebook record available at https://lccn.loc.gov/2022005261

ISBN: 978-1-032-20805-3 (hbk)
ISBN: 978-1-032-21594-5 (pbk)
ISBN: 978-1-003-26911-3 (ebk)

DOI: 10.4324/9781003269113

Typeset in Times New Roman
by Taylor & Francis Books

I dedicate this book to Fred Busch and Daniel Jacobs, with all my love, gratitude, and admiration.

Contents

Permissions

The chapter titled "Un-Translation" is adapted with permission from an article in *Calibán*: Gohar Homayounpour (2015) "Un-Translation." *Calibán, Latin-American Journal of Psychoanalysis*, 13 (1), 140–142.

The chapter titled "Against Empath'ism'" is adapted with permission from a chapter in the book *Mimicry–Empathy*: Gohar Homayounpour (2020) "Against Empath'ism'," in *Mimicry–Empathy*, pp. 200–203. Berlin: Monroe Books.

Preface

The book you are about to read is a strange and out-of-tune collection of unfinished fragments, short stories, very short stories, essays, and...

Persian Blues could be considered a sequel to *Doing Psychoanalysis in Tehran*,[1] so I would like to begin by reminding my readers of what awaits them should they embark upon this psychoanalytic voyage. I wonder if it is possible to genuinely write anything other than sequels? In the pages to come you will re-encounter many of our protagonists from *Doing Psychoanalysis in Tehran*: some will reappear, others will not, and a few will reappear with new disguises. It will remain a carnival of my very own inscription of mourning.

As in *Doing Psychoanalysis in Tehran*, the reader will not find prim-and-proper referencing, with page numbers and close detail. I have attempted, once again, to avoid the defenses which classification and labeling might provide to the flow of the creative act. In this process one finds oneself far from the safety provided by a specific shore, the comfort of the certainties associated with exact categorizing, and the inevitable anxiety that follows in the flow/un-flow of my Blues tune to come.

Persian Blues will follow the same genre of free-associative writing that I formed in *Doing Psychoanalysis in Tehran*, reminiscent of a psychoanalytic session.

The difference is that this time I have dived deeper into the various palettes of the Blues, taking as my departure point the *Isfahan Blues*. In 1963, Duke Ellington went on a famous tour, leading him to Iran, where he played in jazz clubs in Tehran and Isfahan. "Isfahan," named after what most call the most beautiful city in Iran, is a jazz piece credited to Billy Strayhorn and Duke Ellington, and released on Ellington's 1967 album *The Far East Suite*.[2] It features long-time Ellington soloist Johnny Hodges on alto saxophone. (It was originally called "Elf" when Strayhorn composed it, months before the 1963 Ellington Orchestra world tour.)

This "sequel" holds less composition and more improvisation, just like my beloved tunes of the Blues from the Deep South: the sound of the slaves, the lyrics of the laments of ex-slaves and their descendants; it is a genre of music associated with depression, agitation, misfortune, betrayal, pain, and regrets.

And yet we should not forget that the "Blues" also includes raucous dance music that celebrates pleasure, passion, humor, and life. Central to the idea of Blues performance is the concept that, by performing or listening to the Blues, one is able to overcome one's sadness: to lose the "Blues." It is precisely this inherent duality of life and death, Eros and Thanatos, that makes the Blues such a joy to listen to. It is not about merely eroticizing sadness; it is not about drowning in it; it is about transforming it, feeling it, making music with it. Ultimately, it means going beyond the "Blues."

I have often wondered what happened in Isfahan which so allured Duke Ellington that he changed the name of the piece from "Elf" to "Isfahan," considering that in *The Penguin Guide to Jazz*, Richard Cook and Brian Morton suggest that "Isfahan" is arguably the most beautiful item in Ellington's and Strayhorn's entire output.[3] Clearly, I have no idea what really happened, but I imagine that our Blues protagonists were seduced by the various shades of Blue(s) they encountered in Isfahan.

Persian Blue comes in three major tones: Persian Blue proper—a bright medium blue; medium Persian Blue (a slightly grayish mid-blue with faint indigo tones); and a kind of dark blue that is much closer to the web color indigo. Perhaps Ellington's musicians were mesmerized by the blue of some Persian pottery and the color of tiles used in and on mosques and palaces in Iran. Did they find themselves breathless upon entering Naqsh-e Jahan Square (which can be translated as "Image of the World Square") in Isfahan? But perhaps it was just love: maybe Duke Ellington fell in love in Isfahan in 1963.

I endeavored to go deeper and deeper into the Blues: a word associated with melancholia, a mysterious Persian color, and indeed a genre of music which is as much a representation of life as of death, encapsulating triumphs and laments, loss, love, friendships, loyalties, betrayals, joys, fears, and, above all, ambivalence. Hidden within the fathomless endlessness of melancholia, there is nothing but ambivalence.

The deeper I dove, the more I needed my defenses (which led me to insert a couple more essays into the middle of this book). I am an inexperienced diver, but a reasonably good swimmer. For when it comes to the festival of the uncharted underwater, we are indeed swimming blindly. I hope the reader graciously allows me this intake of air: an oxygen tank that you may also find handy at times, as we embark on this strange dive into the map-less undersea, into the "Persian Blues."

I had hoped that the pages that follow would stay faithful to the rhythm of the "Blues": the whole book is an attempt to improvise a Blues song, often out of tune, at times fragmentary, and most definitely in the 12-bar style. The Blues progression has a distinctive form in lyrics, phrasing, chord structure, and duration, so it is not chaos or "anything goes" that I am after: as the reader will hear in the pages to come, I am actually a firm believer in the reality principle... which remains our only possible ticket to arrive at the pleasure principle. In short, we have to psychically give up our concrete sorcerers, our magical thinking, in order to reach their enchantments, to truly access their spells and magic. This I will plunge into repetitively in the coming pages.

The Blues in their predominant form are based on the first, the fourth, and the fifth, but we should never forget that the Blues can be played in any key. The emphasis is not nearly as much on the key as on the player, just as in psychoanalysis. It is not simply what you know but how you use your knowledge, and a constant awareness of what you do not know, that makes you a worthy psychoanalyst. It is not about an accumulation of knowledge. I know somebody (we all know such people) who has the same "hoarding" relationship with money as he does with knowledge, so he piles up money in his bank account and reads at least one book a day, without the slightest ability to use either in a symbolic, meaningful, and pleasurable way. Often in the psychoanalytic seminars that I teach I observe a few candidates who have the same relationship with what Wilfred Bion conceptualized as "–K": negative knowledge, when at the end of the day such a hoarding of knowledge is nothing but a resistance to knowing, to inscribing, to elaborating and having to face the empty space, and to the turbulences that inevitably accompany us on the road to symbolic knowledge.[4] Perhaps we concretely accumulate knowledge, especially in this age of Google and the Internet, devouring information, hoarding supposed knowledge and money, in an unreasonable failed attempt not to face our emptiness, our lack, and ultimately not to entertain the Blues.

I dreamt that this book might follow the notes of the "Blues": where there is music but no melody, where there is improvisation as opposed to composition, since the Blues, like psychoanalysis, belongs to the margins: both are voices from the souls of the underground.

I wish you a turbulent swimming/diving experience; perhaps we might even envision reaching the shore, transformed but alive… we will see, for we are venturing into uncharted waters.

Notes

1 Homayounpour, *Doing Psychoanalysis in Tehran.*
2 Ellington, *Duke Ellington's Far East Suite.*
3 Morton and Cook, *The Penguin Guide to Jazz Recordings.*
4 Jacobus, *The Poetics of Psychoanalysis.*

My Father and I

I remember that night, seven Augusts ago, as if it had just happened; detailed images, sounds, smells and emotions haunt me, but I do not remember a single word after my mother says:

> Come in, sit down, something has happened to your father... he went for a swim today in Lake Leman in Geneva, you know, as he always does when he is visiting your brother in Switzerland in the summer...

Hearing such unnecessary details during this harrowing moment, I lose it, and I shout in the most desperate of wails I have ever heard myself utter: "Is my father dead?" My mother is pretending to be strong and in control, but her shaking hands and the bizarre grayness of her face betray her as she says something I cannot remember, no matter how hard I try, no matter how many times I go back to the details of that night, no matter how many times I relive it in the present and never as an event of the past; every time it is as if it is happening anew, immediate, visceral in the present tense, but I do not remember the words, language fails me in my re-experiencing of that doomed Friday night seven Augusts ago. Instead I vividly remember that my mother's home smelled like its familiar combination of Persian food and Dettol, a strong cleaning material.

That night my husband and I, and my mother's dog, had gone to a party at H's house; it was a strange night from the start: the dog barked all night for no apparent reason, we could not find a parking space for hours so we drove round and round the streets of South Tehran with a barking dog. I was delighted to see AK (a paternal figure for me) at the party; in the bathroom there were two red stilettos, and I was surprised to find out that they were part of the avant-garde decoration of H's new apartment. That evening it had taken me ten minutes to put on my two strands of matching pearls before leaving for H's party.

I remember that night, sitting on the bathroom floor, experiencing a kind of pain that is almost impossible to describe. The first thing I thought was how long it had been since the last time I had spoken with my father, or seen him.

DOI: 10.4324/9781003269113-1

Deep down I knew that I would never again hear his voice; nonetheless I kept calling his number: hoping, wishing, begging that he would pick up and say "Allôoooo...?" with an emphasis on the O.

I thought I would never be able to get up from that bathroom floor. At that very moment, probably as a defense against the unbearableness of it all, in a desperate attempt to find him, to locate him, I Googled Lac Leman:

The first thing I encountered on Google was:

> Falling in love with Lake Geneva is easy... Maybe it's the way the sunlight shimmers on the lake or the way the sunset hits the trees. Or maybe it's the amazing sensation of soaring through the air and laughing with friends on a zip-line adventure, or a fun-filled day on the water...Whatever your choice, Lake Geneva offers events, colors, tastes and wonders for each and every season.[1]

I read and reread that passage until I fell asleep, courtesy of a sleeping pill, on my containing bathroom floor. How vicious and cruel the pearls looked, completely untouched by all that had just occurred. The pearls, uncannily, looked exactly the same, whereas I had been drastically transformed. This was the "Brutality of Things," as the brilliant Italian psychoanalyst Lorena Preta reminds us.[2] *Things* remain the same, while we violently, incessantly change, as we all fall together in time, especially our bodies.

At my father's funeral, from the corner of my eye I saw a woman I did not recognize whispering something to my younger brother that made him turn pale, but I knew that pale face only too well. In the few minutes it took me to leap over to the other side of the room to him, I suddenly remembered that very cold winter day in Ottawa. I was fourteen and he was twelve. He came out of school utterly distressed, telling me that a girl in his class was brutally harassing him. I found the girl immediately and told her if she ever bothered him again she would have me to deal with. She looked shocked, as if there was something I was not aware of, something everybody else knew, that I was missing.

The next day... well, the next day... her sixteen-year-old brother, the toughest footballer in our school, found me and said "I hear you are troubling my sister." I invited him to talk, he reluctantly agreed and at the end of our talk, to my sheer joy he declared that both my brother and I were under his protection from that day on, a promise he kept wholly until he graduated from Woodroffe High School.

This is what my memory is producing, and by the time I reach my pale brother's side at the funeral of my father in Tehran, the unfamiliar woman looks at me and says "I was just telling your brother I hope you had a Muslim burial for your late father in Geneva or his soul will never reach heaven."

Notes

1 Somerton, "Rowing with Annie Vernon at Lake Geneva, Switzerland—Somerton Sporting Club."
2 Preta, *The Brutality of Things.*

Psoriasis

M has patches of psoriasis all over his body.

Medical literature informs us that psoriasis is a disease of the skin in which, for no apparent reason except that it is possibly an autoimmune disorder, skin cells are replaced much more quickly than usual. Essentially, what normally happens in our bodies is that new skin cells take their time to move up through the different layers of skin until they reach the outermost level. This leisurely voyage takes about three to four weeks, then they finally reach their destination, having lived a full and purposeful life. In people with psoriasis, however, the trip for the skin cells is a hurried one, taking only between three and seven days. The cells are therefore an immature and unprepared collectivity that reach their destination on the surface of the body far too quickly, dying before ever getting a chance to really live, causing crusty red patches covered with silvery scales. These skin cells have a tragic, Sisyphean destiny. There is a futile and continuous effort to be useful, to live a full life, but to no avail: faithfully, they never give up on their speedy arrival. If only they would give up on their purpose and stop rushing, if only if they would stand still. Their faithfulness becomes their curse.

Psychoanalysis is my favorite poetic discourse of all time. Yes, when I am asked if I think psychoanalysis is a science or an art, quite apart from the fact that these binary questions are by nature dictatorial (the worst one being when children are asked whether they love their mother or father more), I always respond that psychoanalysis is a poetic discourse. Within this discourse, psoriasis, in many cases, could be linked, it seems, to premature separations.

There it is again, that concept of *premature*: premature skin cells might be the memorial sites of a premature separation, and that is why they repeat the voyage over and over again, each time hoping that the ending will be different. As in everything we repeat in our lives, each time wishing for a different finale, more often than not the ending remains exactly the same. Same scene, different players.

I ask M if he remembers the first time he spotted psoriasis on his skin? "Of course," he says.

DOI: 10.4324/9781003269113-2

I was fourteen years old, and in order to flee obligatory military service in Iran during the Iran–Iraq War, my father sent me to boarding school in France. I remember it intensely: I was in transit alone in Istanbul fleeing the war, when suddenly I saw this patch of red, flaky skin on my knee.

For M, psoriasis showed up on that momentous day in transit through Istanbul not as a curse, but as a "protective shield." People easily forget how protective all of our symptoms can be, how useful for survival. Nevertheless, often surviving, paradoxically, is against living. The superb and original Swiss psychoanalyst Cordelia Schmidt-Hellerau has argued that Freud should have stuck to his first Drive Theory, in which the binary antagonism of the psychic apparatus was between the preservative drive and the life drive, as opposed to his second Drive Theory of Eros and Thanatos, the life and death drives.[1] She finds, if I understand her correctly, that both the preservative drive and the death drive work in the name of tension reduction, so that the mind considers that they belong under the same function. For example, we need sleep to survive, but the moment that we are asleep we are reducing our tension to a point which is the closest thing to a farewell to living which can be experienced in life. Thus all our indispensable survival attempts are closer to death than to life, it seems, and yet without them there would be no life. Could we go as far as to say that all of our symptoms, defenses, particular psychic structures, and pathologies, are *alla fine* merely the best we can do to survive, to not die, not get overwhelmed with tensions, thoughts, and emotions: for the psychic apparatus not to break down? But this vital survival, if it is exaggerated, becomes reminiscent of a culture of the death drive, robbing us of pleasure, desire, and the possibility of developing our own passionate selves.

At that moment in Istanbul, M's skin cells began to work overtime for M's survival. This was probably triggered by the re-experiencing of an earlier premature separation. This new separation triggered an old trauma into coming to the surface, so to speak. Those faithful skin cells, trying to rapidly repair the sense of skinlessness that M was experiencing as he phoned his father from the airport in Turkey.

I can imagine M, with that stunning face, focused, in charge, walking towards that payphone without giving himself the luxury of looking at all those exciting and colorful stores. For a second, seeing a poster of his favorite football player seduces him into slowing down; suddenly he breaks into a surprisingly childish smile, but it quickly disappears into his former strong, distracted, lonely adult gaze. He hurriedly gets to the phone and calls home:

Hello father, everything is fine, don't worry about anything, I have not lost anything and I mailed the letter I was supposed to mail to Paris, I will buy some Turkish delight now, as you advised me, for my host family in France.

His father bursts into tears... but not M, our young, beautiful, determined adolescent boy, who continues: "Father, don't worry about me, I have a list of everything I need to do." From that moment on, "lists" become M's new psychic skin, perhaps as an attempt to compensate for an old failure in his attachments, now fully exposed due to this new site of farewell.

So our hero continues to make lists, and to grow patches of psoriasis, in an attempt to quickly, far too quickly, substitute for never having had the chance to grow a thick skin of his own, appropriately demarcating inside and outside, self and other, external and internal.

M continues to make to-do lists for the next thirty years as his attempt to achieve a psychic container, the actual piece of paper containing these lists having the metaphorical function of a second skin, since for M a typed list on the computer can never carry the same protective psychic function.

***

We know infants are absolutely helpless in the first six months of their lives and absolutely dependent on their caregivers, a helplessness that accompanies us all throughout our lives in the form of a fear and a wish.

For psychoanalysts, many skin conditions may be related to separation–individuation conflicts, and for Freud the first ego is always a body ego.[2] This basically means that the body's exterior is central to human subjectivity and relations. The French psychoanalyst Didier Anzieu posits that the "skin-ego" is a psychic envelope, meaning that the skin, which is originally a shared skin with the mother, is the first ego, the prototype and the building block of our more mature egos to come.[3] So, for Anzieu, our skins are our destiny, and the story of our subjectivity is engraved on our skin, a kind of personalized invisible tattoo. But developing a skin of our own does not happen automatically: we have to achieve it, and any disruptions in this early maternal environment will have disastrous consequences for the history of our becoming.

In my own words, psoriasis is an incomplete mourning, it is a malady of the "blues," because in order to mourn properly we need first to have had our leisurely, shared skin-time with our primary caregiver, we must have our dyadic time where our fantastical delusion that there is no demarcation between our skin and that of the other can be given adequate time: my skin is yours and your skin is mine; it is through this luxurious, hallucinatory wish fulfillment that we can slowly develop the strength to entertain the possibility of such a traumatic but necessary disturbance that we do not share a skin with our mother. As such, if a premature violent separation is introduced before we have had a chance to develop the "blue-print" of a skin of our own and of our egos to come, psoriasis can come to the fore, as a refusal to let go of the beloved object. Psoriasis is a denial of absence.

M's early history is populated with stories of prematurely traumatic separations, never successfully mourned, so on that day when M re-finds himself separating once again in order to flee obligatory military service in the middle of a war, the psychic apparatus is overwhelmed, and it does the only thing that it knows how to do when frightened: it uses the body to deal with this indigestible and alarming material, precisely as we did as helpless infants; we used our body, our only weapon, in an attempt to control it all. Psoriasis came to M's rescue, probing skin cells to start moving quickly in lieu of such a possibility of skinlessness. This, then, is the tragedy of our survival instinct: it comes to the rescue only to prevent us from living, because surviving is indeed often antagonistic to life.

Many years after M's transit event, his father divulged to me: "When my darling son, my only child, called me from the airport that day in transit, I felt like a part of my skin was ripped away from my body forever."

Psoriasis: a memorial site for unfinished mourning; not quite melancholic, just "in transit," and getting to its destination far too quickly.

Notes

1 Schmidt-Hellerau, *Driven to Survive*.
2 Freud, *The Ego and the Id*.
3 Anzieu, *The Skin-Ego*.

Mississippi Blues

At first, the "Blues" might seem to be about the impossibility of transforming the way things are, like the Homeric idea of our hero Odysseus who has to choose between Scylla and Charybdis, which, in Greek mythology, are situated on opposite sides of the Strait of Messina, between Sicily and the Italian mainland. Scylla was a six-headed sea monster and Charybdis was a whirlpool. They were regarded as dangers located so close to each other that together they posed an inescapable threat to passing sailors; avoiding Charybdis meant passing too close to Scylla, and vice versa. According to Homer's account, Odysseus was advised to pass by Scylla and lose only a few sailors, rather than risk the loss of his entire ship in the whirlpool.

What seems at first an impossible choice to Odysseus is really not an impossible one, just an arduous one that will inevitably be accompanied by loss in the name of life: this is the essence of tragedy, as opposed to trauma, which is encapsulated in the belief that the situation we are in, or how we are presently feeling, is going to last forever, that it will always remain as such, that it will never end.

Would it really be a trauma of birth if we could whisper in the newborn's ear that this will last only a few minutes? Or in the midst of depression, after a devastating loss, if only we believed that things will change, that we will one day laugh again, it would not be so traumatic. Trauma is defined by its timelessness.

I am reminded of Julia Kristeva's beautiful assertion in her book *Black Sun*, in which, to put it simply, she asserts that depression starts early and is a pre-Oedipal pathology stemming from the fact that one does not know how to lose the maternal object.[2] "If I did not agree to lose Mother, I could neither imagine nor name her." In short, according to Kristeva, one's Blues come from not knowing how to lose.

Kristeva makes a clear distinction between Dostoyevsky, "the writing of Suffering and forgiveness," an example *par excellence* of the successful sublimation of the "Blues," and the "discourse of dulled pain" expressed by Marguerite Duras.[3]

DOI: 10.4324/9781003269113-3

Dostoyevsky is able to verbalize the effect of suffering in a new style. For Kristeva, Dostoyevsky's writing achieves the transformation of melancholia that best encapsulates how the "unconscious might inscribe itself in a new narrative that will not be the eternal return of the death drive."[4] Unlike Dostoyevsky, Duras' "discourse of dulled pain" captures the "malady of death" in "an aesthetics of awkwardness" and "a non-cathartic literature," a style which is certainly less musical than our "Blues" genre. As Kristeva writes:

> There is no purification in store for us at the conclusion of those novels written on the brink of illness, no improvement, no promise of a beyond, not even the enchanting beauty of style or irony that might provide a bonus of pleasure in addition to the revealed evil.

For Kristeva, Duras' writing, unlike Dostoyevsky's, demonstrates her inability to sublimate her "passion for death." Kristeva goes on:

> Duras does not orchestrate [the malady of suffering] in the fashion of Mallarmé, who sought for the music in words, nor in the manner of Beckett, who refines a syntax that marks time or moves ahead by fits and starts, warding off the narrative's flight forward.

My beloved genre of the "Blues" belongs to the Dostoyevskian tradition of melancholia, always imprinted with transcriptions, music, words, pleasure, creativity, and dance in a collectivity of listeners together trying to stay clear of the seductive powers of the pure culture of the death drive, if it were possible to entertain such a purity *à la* Duras. Within the Blues, there is always the chance of a pleasurable beyond.

The "Blues," just like psychoanalysis, is the music of the margins, subversive by definition, and the moment either one becomes mainstream it loses its *raison d'être*; certainly the Blues could come only from African Americans of the Deep South. Psychoanalysis, as Mariano Horenstein asserts, is a process of foreignization which came from the border and belongs to foreigners, and to the foreigner within each of us.[5] Horenstein elaborates:

> The place of the foreigner is a disillusioning place—not as inert or melancholic since it is there where desire nests and enthusiasm is fostered—but disillusioning with regard to any tempting ideal of belonging, even in an analytic affiliation.[6]

So maybe it is not belonging for which we should search, but Un-belonging: immigrants and refugees should not assimilate, or rid themselves of their accents and foreignness; they should inflict on us their foreignness, the very "thing" we are the most phobic of.

In an age when we are dealing with a crisis of immigration and refugees, it becomes more significant than ever to unpack this idea of "foreignness." At a seminar I was attending in Berlin on immigration and refugees, during a clinical report on a group therapy, there was a delightful moment for all of us as we came face-to-face with a Syrian woman who said to the group therapist: "You are too skinny, you are not eating well, you know this German food is absolutely horrible; I will bring you some baklava next time." Without going into the various possible psychoanalytic interpretations of such a communication, there was something deeply refreshing and deconstructionist about this dialogue. It was refreshing because it fights clichés. Because it is subversive. At times I feel the danger of falling into the trap of "reality" in working with such groups: that the brutal reality of it will seduce us all into leaving our analytic positions, in order to "do" something. At times this is a defense against the inevitable helplessness of such a real, cruel situation. But analysts are not social workers, they are not psycho-pharmacologists, they are not humanists, they don't necessarily even have to be good people, in my unpopular opinion. But they are nomads, marginal, and always in search of the unconscious. This, to me, is not a vision of psychoanalysis that can be compromised: not in the name of infantilizing our patients to death, not in the name of being really kind and good, and not in the name of a politically correct discourse of our time.

Notes

1 Horenstein, *The Compass and the Couch*.
2 Kristeva, *Black Sun*.
3 Kristeva, "The Pain of Sorrow in the Modern World: The Works of Marguerite Duras," 140.
4 Kristeva, "On the Melancholic Imaginary."
5 Horenstein, "Psychoanalysis in Minor Language."
6 Horenstein, *The Compass and the Couch*.

If They Go Away

Suddenly, during the Berlin congress mentioned above, I had an anxious association to an article I had recently read, entitled "Things Are So Bad in Iran that Afghan Migrants Are Going Home."[1] In Iran, the largest immigrant population we have had since our country opened its borders in 1979 to refugees from the Soviet war has been the Afghan community, with over three million arrivals, and now things are economically so bad in Iran that even they are leaving in their thousands, waiting at the borders to attempt to get back to Afghanistan. This "reverse migration" is the result of American sanctions against Iran imposed in 2018, which have led to an economic crisis and a huge deflation of the Iranian currency. It means that working and living in Iran is no longer worth it for most Afghan immigrants, who traditionally used to send a large part of their salary to their families in Afghanistan.

At times, perhaps, in the midst of the vast triumphs of right-wing governments in various countries, including some with fascist politics and policies, whose successful populist discourse so often, at some level, has to do with the flux of immigrants and refugees; at a time when we often hear "It is too much, we have taken too many people in, what about other countries? They have to take their share; are these immigrants and refugees ruining our cities, are they stealing our jobs…?" To all of these questions I want to answer: things are so bad in Iran that even Afghan immigrants are leaving.

Does this not say it all? They come in their thousands to your land because you have something to offer them so that they can survive. This is a clear sign of prosperity and possibility. Embrace it as such, because the day might come when they will leave because you are in a depletion crisis of your own. I felt jealous of these host countries. They were wondering how to deal with this influx, and I was haunted, tormented by the title of this article.

It is my wish to use the specific example of reverse migration by Afghan immigrants in Iran which is so strikingly shown in Bahman Kiarostami's documentary film *Exodus* in order to deconstruct the current clichés and dangerous discourses on immigration that have led to such catastrophic conditions on a global scale.[2] I attempt to bring a new elaboration to it, trying to stay away from the current binary approaches which I might formalize as

DOI: 10.4324/9781003269113-4

either humanitarian or fascist, master or slave, oppressor or oppressed, and moving towards a discourse beyond good and evil.

The term "reverse migration"—which, remarkably, is also known as "misorientation"—is a phenomenon in bird migration when a bird flies in the opposite direction of what is species-typical during the migration period.

"Internal reverse human migration," then, has to do with people moving back to rural life from more urban, cosmopolitan cites, often motivated by the depletion of big cities and all the problematics that come with living in these urban areas. These depletions might include pollution, expensive housing, a lack of good job opportunities, and so on. In short: a trend toward reverse migration in any shape or form, either internal or external, is a clear and unquestionable sign of depletion and a lack of prosperity in the place that people are leaving behind.

Thus, when we see a trend toward reverse human migration, we can take it as a clear sign of the host country or city's diminution par excellence. In the same way, when you leave me, it is bound to produce anxiety in me, since your leaving is a clear sign of my depletion. Hence your departure is disorienting/misorienting.

This anxiety is palpable in a few scenes of Kiarostami's documentary, including the beginning sequence in *Exodus*, when the voice of the director is heard from behind the camera asking an Afghan worker who is bidding farewell to his friend if he also plans to leave Iran?

What I find marvelous about *Exodus* is that the camera is not situated in a way that allows us to identify with either the Afghans or the Iranian authorities; the boundaries between subject and object, victim and aggressor, are blurred, precisely disturbing us, disorienting us into taking a different route. A route which is unlike the politically correct route we see advertised and promoted these days more than ever before; the politically correct discourse which I would even go so far as to call the diagnosis of the spirit of the times.

When it comes to this politically correct discourse, which is centered around guilt, safety, and infantilization of the Other, I would like to propose a "reverse migration" for all of us from the status quo towards which everyone else is flying. It is true that it is hard for birds who lose their flock and their way to survive, but for the few who make it through this reverse migration, it will allow them to land in a space of "thinking thoughts."

So neither the discourse of "these poor immigrants and refugees," or that of "we are tired of taking so many in," represents the real question here. The real question means penetrating into the very issue which has been so well elaborated within the reverse immigration of Afghan people in Iran: that when they leave, god help us; that is the moment when we are in trouble, when a drought is foreshadowed. And all I want to sing for these Afghan immigrants, with the help of Frank Sinatra, is: "Please don't go away."[3]

Reverse migration is disorienting, as watching *Exodus* is, and I believe some of the intense controversy Bahman Kiarostami has provoked in Iran is precisely for this reason. Certainly, we must also acknowledge that these phenomena are clearly multilayered.

Moreover, the anxiety is palpable within a dialectical tension between the audience and *Exodus*, between the object and the subject. For me, watching it was like watching the play of *Oedipus Rex*. As Freud says, we know the ending, but every time we watch the play, we wish that the ending could be different: in this case that they will stay; that they will not leave; that they will think there is a chance they will come back... not, as some critics of the documentary have suggested, in order for us to continue our abuse of our slaves, nor because suddenly Iranians, with their long history of mistreating Afghan immigrants in many shapes and forms, have suddenly transformed into humanitarians: our anxiety is significantly deeper than that.

The master–slave dynamic is deconstructed and constructed right before our eyes; the power dynamic is suddenly reversed, leaving us disoriented... if you stay, it means that I will find a way to survive, to master the drought, but if you leave and never come back, it is a clear sign that I am doomed forever, ill-fated to experience an attack on my own existence, without any possibility of survival.

So if you stay, I will do my darnedest to make you a day, to make us a day... like none that we have ever lived. In the final analysis, this has to do with love and loss, with impoverished egos, with life and death, the drive to survive, and the very structure of desire. This picture, this very picture I am presenting, that *Exodus* is presenting, is to disorient you into a different way of seeing how lucky you are that there is a flux of immigrants and refugees wanting to come to your land. For, to paraphrase the song, if they go away they will take the sun... there will be nothing to fill up our hands... just an empty space and an empty gaze. All your resources will be just for you... until your lonely death, in a depleted desert of your own.[4]

It is not immigrants and refugees who deplete us, it is that when they leave, their departure itself is a sign of our *a priori* depletion. Their arrival is a sign of our vitality: welcome them, for in this non-humanitarian hospitality we are greeting our own sense of aliveness.

The usual familiar discourses around immigration focus on those who desperately want to enter our lands, not on their exits. I believe that along these lines we can bring new elaborations, much needed at this particular time, into this particular discourse.

Notes

1 Radio Free Europe / Radio Liberty, "Things Are So Bad in Iran that Afghan Migrants Are Going Home."
2 RIDM, *Exodus*.
3 Sinatra, *If You Go Away*.
4 Sinatra, *If You Go Away*.

The Forgotten War

The Iran–Iraq War has been referred to as the "Forgotten War," even though it was one of the longest and bloodiest of the twentieth century. It was an armed conflict between Iran and Iraq, beginning in 1980, when Iraq invaded Iran, and ending on 20 August 1988, when Iran accepted the UN-brokered ceasefire. Iraq wanted to replace Iran as the dominant state in the Persian Gulf, and was worried that the 1979 Iranian Revolution would lead Iraq's Shi'ite majority to rebel against the Ba'athist government.

Although Iraq hoped to take advantage of Iran's post-revolutionary chaos, it made limited progress and was quickly repelled; Iran regained virtually all lost territory by 1982, two years after the war started. The United States, the Soviet Union, France, and most Arab countries provided political support for Iraq, while Iran was largely isolated.

By the end of the war, nearly eight years later, more than a million people were dead, and both countries deeply wounded.

This sounds uncannily familiar, for it is exactly where we find ourselves in 2021, with increasing tensions between the USA and Iran, and continual threats of military action on both sides since the Trump administration unilaterally pulled out of the nuclear accord, formally known as the Joint Comprehensive Plan of Action, or JCPOA, which saw the USA and other powers—France, Germany, the United Kingdom, China, and Russia—lift certain economic sanctions in exchange for Iran accepting limits on and inspections of its nuclear program.

Everyone says that neither side wants war, but if we look at history, didn't most wars start by accident? How can we forget the Iran–Iraq War when most political analysts univocally agree that it has marked the politics of the Middle East ever since, in what Iran still to this day calls the "Imposed War" or the "Wholly Defensive War." In an article from the *Guardian* (23 September 2010), Ian Black describes the covert support of the West for Saddam Hussein, from US satellite evidence of Iranian military movement to European armament supplies:

> Iran's continuing suspicions of America and Europe cannot be understood without remembering that grim period. Washington wanted both countries to bleed, but it feared Iran more.[1]

DOI: 10.4324/9781003269113-5

As Black shows, Saddam Hussein's rapid progress across the oil-rich Khuzestan region and into Khorramshahr was too much, too fast, leaving Iraq over-exposed. At the same time, the Iraqi leader was trying, in vain, to assume a prominent role across the Arab world: the nearest he got was significant financial support from the Gulf states for the war.

Meanwhile, as Black points out, Iran was able to mobilize out of a population almost three times that of Iraq's, and put Iraq onto the back foot by mid-1982. Iraq wasn't able to conclusively shift the development of the conflict for over six years, as the death toll mounted swiftly to "an estimated one million for Iran and 250,000–500,000 for Iraq."[2]

As Black demonstrates, the long and bloody conflict seemed "like a forgotten war" in the West, one that has shrunk in historical analyses against later wars where Western powers played a more prominent role: "Iraq's invasion of Kuwait in 1990 and the US-led invasion and occupation of 2003 which overthrew Saddam Hussein and changed the political map of the region."

> But for those directly involved, memories of the Iran–Iraq war can still be raw and painful.[3]

One of those directly involved is A. She remembers it with every grain of her being, more than thirty years after the end of the war, and after literally thirty operations on her father, whose leg was severely injured and who had to have a new hip replacement just yesterday. And A, once again, had to clean her father's blood from the bathroom floor.

A is a psychology professor. Let us say we share a passion for deep diving… she has been trying to remember/forget, just like everyone else in the world…

I vividly remember the first dream she reported to me, right at the beginning of our friendship: there was a whore in her dream with very exaggeratedly long nails and horrible make-up; she was vulgar, and she was trying to seduce A into joining her line of work. In the dream, A is both scared and intrigued. Well, it does not take a sophisticated analyst to figure out who the whore might be. "I," the Western-educated, improperly veiled woman, the Freudian analyst. Especially because she was teaching psychology, interested, after all, in my line of psychoanalytic work. Yes, certainly I / the whore also represents a projected part of herself, one that both intrigues and scares her. The very part of herself that she has gone to a psychoanalytic couch of her own to encounter, yet is terrified of that very meeting. Thus it took many years of not challenging her whorish image of me before A slowly, cautiously, came to recognize it in herself.

She has rightly been very mistrustful of me from the beginning. I represented an encapsulation of the "Other Side"…

Yesterday she dreamt that she was trying to get a ticket to India. India has associations of its own for her. She traveled there a few years ago, and she loved it: she felt free, close to nature, a certain peace... she loved the stories of Indian gods... if one god did not listen to you, and your prayers were not answered, you could beat them furiously and then leave that particular god for a better god; she laughed wholeheartedly when she was telling me this story. But instead of India, in her dream she ends up in Gom (the most religious city in Iran, associated with religious schools and highly devout people). She continues:

> After my father's last operation last week, when he really looked like Gandhi [there, I think, is the India connection] you know, so thin, he has lost ten kilos, and he was only fifty-five kilos to begin with... well, you know his friends were there to visit him, and they were talking about everything that is going on in society; the poverty, the corruption, the Mafia-ness of it all, the social class gap getting wider and wider; my father, who never cried, no matter how much physical pain he has been in ever since he was injured in the war, when he almost lost his leg and had to get a fake hip: he started crying yesterday...
>
> His friends asked him: "Why are you crying? You are a soldier of God, you who went to war to protect this land and to defend so many lives..."
>
> My father, still crying, replied: "I went into this war not because I was forced to go, for I believed ideologically in the Revolution that we had made, I believed in taking back the rights of the people, I believed in its socialist ideals. I was an orphan, you know, the most forgotten group in any society, I entered the war voluntarily and now I don't know why I did it any more. What if all my thirty-something operations were senseless? What if we were wrong?"
>
> His friend replied: "We were attacked unfairly by Iraq and Saddam Hussein, they wanted to take advantage of us, men like you were patriotic, you defended Iran and Iranians, the Iran–Iraq War was beyond ideology."

A contributed to their conversation, saying:

> But, to this day, it seems like it was the war of the poor: mostly poor and religious people went to war and fought for this country, got injured, gave their lives, we paid the price and now that we have certain benefits via the "Bonyad janbazan va mostazafan" [The Foundation of the Oppressed, Disabled and Martyrs]; it makes me livid, fuming, when the very same people whose lives and land we defended are resentful of the benefits we receive, and say: "Oh, did you use your ever-bountiful subsidies to get into university? It's not really fair, you take our children's well-deserved places at the universities."

A continues:

> I want to yell at such people, to ask them: Where were you when my father was not around to do my homework with me? Where have you been for the last thirty years? I spend at least three hours of my day taking care of his physical needs: I have been putting my father's socks on for the past thirty years, I do the grocery shopping for the house, I was nine months old when he got injured and he was in the hospital for almost a year with one operation after another and endless infections... my mother would put on a mask and fully cover herself to take care of him at the hospital and then she would come and breastfeed me, terrified that she was giving me infected milk. After all of this, when I visit the affluent North Tehran shops, I am completely humiliated by their degrading attitude; is it because I wear the chador? What do you think, Gohar?

I am reminded of so many dinner parties with those of my social class, saying exactly what she is complaining about. They often say: "They took our kids' places in the universities because they have an advantage over them with their 'subsidies'." How many times have I heard them say, "I am disgusted by anyone who wears the chador."

Just the other day I overheard someone saying: "Now even on the beaches of the south of France I have to see these completely veiled women, nowhere to run to." So I know that A is right, and I am as furious as she is about these comments... how many fights and arguments I have gotten into over the years...

A angrily goes on:

> And since these foundations are exempt from taxes, they are continually criticized as a major weakness in the Iranian economy, tapping off production to the lucrative black market, while doing their job inadequately. The existence of such foundations is also under attack, for not really helping the poor but only benefiting allies of the government, while unfairly confiscating people's property, and tampering with the creation of a proper social security system in Iran.

She looks me straight in the eyes and says:

> I am not idealizing these foundations; some of these accusations are correct, nobody knows that better than I do. But I am a specific example, a living proof: they have been indispensable to my family and me. Promise me you will tell my story at one of your dinner-party gatherings in North Tehran, where affluent women try to reduce their guilt with stupid charities like buying computers for street girls and providing dance classes—

> ha-ha!—dance classes for street girls, yes, that's what they need. Maybe these women should volunteer at one of these foundations. That would be charity, that would be eye-opening, maybe even transformative.

I say to her:

> I don't have an answer to your question, I'm not sure why you are treated as you say you are in some parts of the city because you are fully veiled, but I think your father deserves a medal for what he has done for this country. I wish for you to believe in my deep gratitude and convey it to him.

She says "Thank you," adding, in her usual sarcastic tone of voice, "The rich sent their boys to boarding schools abroad in order for them to flee military service; those poor thin-skinned boys, the separation must have been quite traumatic for them."

After listening to A, I think how forgetting about wars is certainly less a memory lapse as much as it is about the fact that the forgetting allows us to repeat—or do we, as Freud said, repeat because we have attempted to forget? We repeat as a compromise between remembering and forgetting. Or maybe the answer is to be found in an almost forgotten correspondence between Freud and Einstein on "Why War?"

It is quite daunting how it could be applied verbatim to our situation today, and also how this significant correspondence has been "forgotten," repressed.

By the time the exchange between Einstein and Freud was published in 1933, under the title *Why War?*, Hitler, who was to drive both men into exile, was already in power, and the letters never achieved the wide circulation for which they had been intended. Indeed, the first German edition of the pamphlet is reported to have been limited to only 2,000 copies, as was the original English edition.

***

A, who seems calmer now, goes on to elaborate on why she experiences her own strong ambivalence toward these foundations. It is very hard for her to digest that she is indebted to those very people who took her father away from her, as the organizations that help her and her family, such as the Foundation for Martyrs and Veteran Affairs, have helped them for over thirty years, but this help is contingent upon a confirmation of being a *majrooh* [injured], an injured person. The first question asked upon entering the foundation is: "To what percent are you injured?" The higher the percentage of the injury, the more bountiful the aid package.

I think at this point how vividly A is elaborating a general problematic of the wilting liberal/humanitarian discourse, for a discourse of compensation is always a discourse of injury and victimhood: I will help you out, as soon as we confirm that you are an injured party; my help will transform you into an injured party along the way.

A goes on:

> Can you believe it, my mother said to me the other day, we are lucky your father has a seventy-five percent injury; I wanted to kill her. We are lucky that he is so ill, isn't this perverse, in your psychoanalytic language? And yet I am indeed indebted to those very people now who took my father away; the raw ugly truth is that I have gotten breaks every step of the way because of my father's injuries.

I am reminded yet again of the disgust associated with the name of these foundations within the same veil-hating group of society, how difficult it is to digest it all. It seems that the "in-digestible" is our uncomfortable companion wherever we go nowadays. Each group is splitting and projecting a part of themselves they cannot digest into the other group. And this allows each group to avoid dealing with the inevitable ambiguities of their being.

I am reminded that when a very loving American colleague wrote me a letter of apology on behalf of her government (the Trump administration), I found the experience indigestible, because I was supposed to feel gratitude for her kindness and sweetness. Alas, she is the most giving and kind analyst. Once, she told me in the name of empathy, she let a patient who had lost her home stay with her temporarily; she is the sweetest of them all... yet all I felt upon receiving her letter of apology was anger. I felt somehow offended.

I am willing to entertain the possibility that I am no more than an ungrateful person who turns people's sweet apologetic gestures into offences, and should recommend more psychoanalysis for myself: that is certainly a probability. Yet what I felt was: how grandiose of her to apologize on behalf of her nation; also, I think that within this apology she is turning me into an injured and victimized party, rather like the Foundation for Martyrs and Veteran Affairs did to A. At that moment I become the injured party and she the humanitarian dispensing aid. At the very moment of her apology, she "named" me.

I find it indigestible when I realize that my socio-political positions align me with the very people I have critiqued all my life: for example, like any thinking being I am very critical of the Iranian government, yet when the Trump administration is the one backing out of the nuclear deal, while the Iranian side has kept its end of the bargain, I can assure you I am on the Iranian government's side, yet this very position dislocates me, this very position is indigestible indeed.

And when everybody in the Trump administration was clapping for war, except Donald Trump himself, I found an ally in Trump, and how indigestible that is...

And when it drives me mad that Saudi Arabia can brutally kill dissident journalist Jamal Khashoggi, and when the world agrees that the Crown Prince of Saudi Arabia should be investigated over this murder because there is "credible evidence" that he and other senior officials were responsible for the killing, according to a damning and forensic UN report, and what happens instead is that the USA sells a billion-plus of weapons to Saudi Arabia, well...

Yet all these social/liberal positions of mine become lost to me when the good people of a social/liberal persuasion preach about the politically correct and send letters of apology.

And when everything associated with sex, especially within university campuses, has become about danger and disease. Once upon a time, pleasure—oh that strange un-liberal notion of pleasure—was allied with sex. In my non-social/liberal outlook I have come to think of the politically correct as the new authoritarianism of our times. It seems surprising, but is it so surprising after all?

It was in this same geography of political correctness that *Fifty Shades of Grey* (2011),[4] the first novel in a trilogy of sadomasochistic erotica about a dominating young executive by Erika Mitchell Leonard (aka E.L. James), topped the bestseller lists, followed by *Fifty Shades Darker* and *Fifty Shades Freed*.[5] At the same time, and in the same vein, the (failed?) American dream chose Donald Trump, with his scandalous use of misogynist language and allegations of misconduct toward women, as its democratically elected president. Keeping all this data in mind, one is left wondering whether this might be the expression of an unconscious collective desire to free oneself from submission to a politically correct discourse, a desire which is then projected onto an external vehicle such as Donald Trump. The timely appeal of James' story of submission and domination encapsulates the complexities of the feminine soul, with millions of women being "seduced" by this sadomasochistic erotica, which became "the fastest adult novel to sell one million copies in paperback, smashing previous record holders, *The Da Vinci Code* and *Harry Potter*."[6]

It is important to note that James' *Fifty Shades of Grey* has extensive appeal for female readers, and that its fans are mostly comprised of married women over thirty: a clue which led some critics to call it the "Mommy Porn" of the day. Along these lines, it is also significant to take a look at new statistics from contemporary Britain, where a considerable number of women prefer to remain housewives, married to rich husbands. Should we not take a critical and psychoanalytic look at these contemporary phenomena? The feminine soul is experiencing turbulence, for good or for bad, and in order to envision the possibility of a safe landing, we need our "psychoanalytic mind."[7] We cannot settle for concrete solutions, for the misleading concreteness that is epitomized within the politically correct is reminiscent of the concreteness of totalitarian regimes. To return to the symptomology of

political correctness: as well as the politics against it, I would like to praise...
well, in short, there are quite a few "incorrectnesses" within various politically
correct discourses of our times. If these matters are not assessed carefully, we
are in danger of falling into new forms of authoritarianism: the same ideolo-
gies in different guises. These new forms of authoritarianisms are not only
hazardous for all, but also deadeningly boring.

I was talking to a Saudi friend and an Israeli friend at lunch. I will spare
the reader all the actual politically incorrect jokes we were making, but this
Israeli friend, who is an old-school leftist, has three sons, two of whom have
been imprisoned in Israel for refusing to go into the military.

I asked her what Noah (her youngest) was planning to do? She said: "He'll
be here in ten minutes, ask him yourself." This clean-cut boy with kind, deep
blue eyes showed up, so I asked him. He said:

> I refuse to join a compulsory military, and I will go to prison instead,
> because this is the answer to ending war that Einstein requested from
> Freud; have you read it? They had a beautiful correspondence. If no one
> joins, the military will be forced to find another fucking thing to do with
> our innate destructiveness.

The non-humanitarian in me got up and hugged him: an Iranian, a Saudi,
and an Israeli (it sounds like the beginning of a joke) with their nations at
war, but here at lunch, old friends together, we saw a glimpse of an answer
through Noah's determination not to join the military.

My Saudi friend Latifa, a friend from high school, has mastered the art of
making all the un-digestibility of motherhood comical. She drinks quite a bit
of wine, and admits to shouting at her children often, to wanting to abandon
them all, to having been shocked at her body's transformation during her
pregnancies, and—most ambivalently—to the never-discussed horrors/joys of
breastfeeding. (God bless her: she has three children.) So one day, our very
sophisticated childless friend asked her: "OK, you had one because you
wanted children, and then you had the second one so the first wouldn't be
alone, but why the third one? Children are like savages."

Latifa could not agree more with our friend; and she told him:

> But you know, what is more savage than kids themselves is the whole
> perverse discourse around maternity, which starts with women being
> asked, usually by other women, "Was it a natural birth or a C-section?
> Did you use an epidural, or did you do it naturally? Did you breastfeed?
> And for how long? Why did you go back to work so early? If you must go
> back to work so early, at least don't go to the gym so often..."
>
>   Insisting that it was worth all the pain, physical transformations, and
> the real risks which actually becoming pregnant imposes on a woman's
> body... and above all, as a mother you should not even have impure

thoughts. Forget about a sexual life; even the thought of it is forbidden. So, in short:

"How come you still have a life of your own?"

To this tyranny of naturalism, Latifa always responded: "Then go to the dentist without any anesthesia…" According to her, the more masochistic one is, the more the image of a virtuous mother is portrayed to a gleeful audience; a discourse of maternity has always been a discourse of crime and punishment, and one which is particularly highlighted within the relationship of mothers and daughters.

Latifa has always asserted that patriarchy and society in general are what fail mothers first and foremost, but a transgenerational relationship between women is certainly at work as well, and both of these collude to create what she calls the perverse discourse of maternity.

Latifa's three children are some of the freest, most interesting and loving subjects I have encountered…

Her oldest daughter once told me this story:

> When I was three or four years old, mommy used to play with me and my infamous stuffed bunny, Maria Elena, and often she would say: Elena the good bunny, Elena the bad bunny… always remember, my darling girl, that it is the same bunny! Good and bad, she is our Elena and we love her… good bunny, bad bunny… it is the same bunny.

Latifa wholeheartedly respects her children's right to privacy and secrets, for one of the cruelest and most gruesome crimes we can commit against another is to demand to know everything about them, not to allow them secrets of their own. Psychoanalysts have to be particularly cautious of such crimes. To love, just like transference in the analytic relationship, implies having secrets.

My dear friend would be the first person to tell you that it is not that she has figured out the secret or the recipe for motherhood. She does not believe there is one to be found, as she aptly put it the other day:

> The only thing I am sure of about motherhood is that it will test all your limits to the core, and then some… and my only weapon has been to try, often in vain, every day, to give up my power.

That is her line of ethics: a politics of transforming power relations, not easily achievable, impossible to arrive at completely.

I remember that when she called me after my father's death, she told me: "I still haven't forgiven the group of women who showed up with their perfect make-up and, oh, those coordinated pearl necklaces to my father's funeral." I said: Oh, my dear Latifa, I have had worse encounters; someone came to me at my father's funeral and said: "I am so sorry for what you are going through; if I lost my father I would kill myself." Latifa, shocked, asked: "What did you say?" I said: You should start organizing your suicide now, for he will certainly die one day; everybody dies, you know. Latifa, my dear gentle friend, laughed; we laughed together, and then she said: "You didn't say that, but you should have." I replied: I thought it, I thought it.

Dana, my Israeli friend, stays faithful to her name (Dana is a Hebrew name meaning "arbiter" or "God is my judge") and repeatedly judges, and that's another reason we all love her. She continues over our lunch:

> These social-liberal clichés about motherhood! Can you believe it: last night an acquaintance—I refuse to call her a friend, for as Milan Kundera says, the one and only thing one should accept from one's friends is to be polite with them—this acquaintance from San Francisco made me feel guilty because I don't have my own chickens in my back yard, and I feed my grown-up children supermarket-bought eggs.

I say: You have two sons in prison and your third, god willing, on his way there, and she judges you for not feeding your kids home-grown eggs!

Latifa says:

> My kids had a birthday party the other day, and two mothers asked me if the fruit was organic, for if not her kids would not eat it. I wanted to hit her on the head with the non-organic watermelon: do you think I need psychiatric meds, Gohar?

I say: You know, Freud said we have children out of our own sense of narcissism, reaching for immortality, and he was absolutely right. Listen to all of us saying oh, he has my grandmother's eyes, my own smile, obsessing over that possessive adjective "my"... Parents are fixated on these remarks, yet I think having a child is also one of the most narcissistically injurious events of our lives. I had fantasies all my life that I would be such a cool bohemian mother, the wise psychoanalyst mother, how I would judge all mothers on so many things they did, and back then I judged them with such ease. All my judgments came back to haunt me as soon as I became a mother, because karma is merciless, my dear friends.

My maternal Blues is deep, beautiful, musical, with big black eyes, a peach-colored skin, and eyelashes so long you could spend long summer days swinging from them.

The melody of the Blues carries us... I kept listening to classical music while I was pregnant with her, but she is a Blues kind of girl, and she was from the very beginning.

When they handed her to me, I wondered: What the hell am I going to do with her?... I wanted to stay in the hospital forever, marry the pediatrician (just because he was a pediatrician, at that moment any pediatrician would have done) to help me raise her and check on her, and answer all my questions. But to my surprise, when I shared with Dr. Philip my desire to marry him, he said, "I would never marry a psychoanalyst," and abruptly left the room...

I knew that I would never shout at her, I would never compare her to other children, I would never impose my desires on her, I would never fight with my husband in front of her, I would never make her compete for grades, attend extracurricular activities which she did not want to attend, and a thousand other "I would nots."

My dear friends, I did all those things, every single one, and more than once, and felt guilty because I was a working mother and, secretly, not the playing-with-dolls kind of mother.

I thought that I knew better, I thought that I was very aware of the uselessness of guilt, I thought I knew not to buy into these clichéd ideas around perfect, loving mothers, magnificently elaborated in Jacqueline Rose's book with the superb title *Mothers, an Essay on Love and Cruelty*.[8] I fell into all the traps of motherhood, every single one, and oh my, it was a blow to my narcissism indeed. I was as delusional as it gets when it came to being a mother.

And with my daughter I felt the melodramatic feelings that I had managed to keep away from after many years of analysis.

I love my Ocean Blues: yes, I named her Darya, which means the sea. She came to me after my father's death, after his heart gave up while he was swimming...

Jacqueline Rose elaborates:

> If you are asking mothers to be perfect, why wouldn't they pass that impossible demand on to their child? Any mother who obeys this diktat could therefore be said to be perversely fulfilling the requirements of her role. Perfection breeds perfection, lives frozen at the core, compulsively fawning over themselves (it is surely no coincidence that perfection is also the false promise of consumer objects, every disappointing purchase leads to the next).

Basically, she asserts that what has historically been wrongfully demanded of mothers has been to be good and only good, to just be mothers and nothing else, and definitely not to be sexual beings; that is a major sin. She goes on to say that "mothers do not have a monopoly of love in the world."

Dana says: "But, Gohar, Winnicott, the famed British psychoanalyst, says mothers just have to be good enough."

I say:

> But Winnicott is the one who makes me feel the guiltiest of all: his good-enough, ordinary mother who, according to him, does not even need to be educated, for all of this will come naturally to her. Winnicott's good-

enough mother is a perfect combination of natural maternal instinct, enough love and care, not suffocating, with the capacity to be alone and the capacity to hate. Oh, and we mustn't forget to be natural, spontaneous, and funny.

It is true that in his pioneering article on "Hate in the Counter-Transference" Winnicott introduces the usefulness of hate in any relationship—mother and child, psychoanalyst and analysand, elaborating: "If, for fear what she may do, she cannot hate appropriately when hurt by her child, she must fall back on masochism... the baby needs hate to hate... and sentimentality is useless for parents."[9] He even goes on to list eighteen reasons why a mother would hate her baby from the start. All brilliant, and a significant contribution, but at times it is contradictory, as even within the Winnicottian discourse one is, in my opinion, continually confronted with the very maternal sentimentality and naturalness that he is advocating against elsewhere.

Every single day I thank Darya for coming into my world, and mean it with a certainty that I lack in most avenues in my life. And I tell her silently: I promise to contain you via providing limits... to love you, to hate you, to try to respect you and wish for you to do the same. For respect is quite different from being educated and loving. And I beg her to at least be partially a slave to my desire; god knows I am often certainly one to hers, and never give up on working toward each of us having free minds of our own.

I have come to think that it is fundamental for both mother and child to believe that their aggression for each other will not destroy either. I told my friends this story, that the other day I had asked Darya to drink her orange juice and she said no. I said OK, and continued what I was doing, then she looked at me and said: "Are you crying because I didn't drink my orange juice?" to which I responded: My darling, I love you very much, but your orange-juice drinking is not so vital that it will make me cry if you don't drink it. We both laughed together to my response; there was a wonderful sense of freedom and playfulness, as if she became free at the moment that my love for her had limits. Limitless love is the most horrifying experience one can impose on a child—on anybody, really. And to be the unlucky recipient of such limitless love is like a death sentence for the psyche of that very child.

Latifa, gentle Latifa, says:

Oh, Gohar you are too comically hard on yourself, you have so much respect for the Oedipus complex it makes me feel dizzy. You know what my mother did with my erotic, feminine side? I will never forget it: It was a friend's *bal masqué* birthday party. I was eight years old and I had dressed up as Madonna, the famous sexy singer, and felt very attractive. The host asked everyone to dance, announcing that the best dancer would receive a prize. I waited, and shyly entered the dance floor as the last competitor. I felt everyone's gaze upon me; my friends and the host's mother were shockingly pleased, so I became courageous and let go, started dancing like I had never danced before. The host called my mother to join us from the living room where the mothers were chatting: "Come in and see how exquisitely your daughter is dancing!" I continued proudly under my mother's gaze, downright enamored with myself, almost in a trance. Suddenly my mother turned to the host and said: "My poor girl is pretending; she is really not a dancer."

I felt so humiliated, I wanted to run out of there as quickly as possible and never show my face again. The worst part was that I was really at the height of desire, pleasure, and the newly awakened eroticism in a young girl just coming out of the latency period. And here was my forbidding maternal superego with a clear intolerance for the erotic pleasure that I was experiencing. After such a command, one is bound to feel guilty (I have internalized her voice, my mother's command not to enjoy): every time you experience pleasure you have to punish yourself in the monarchy of the superego which reigns over us without mercy, just like the Queen of Hearts in *Alice in Wonderland* (Ha! the cruelest part of the superego is a queen, not a king, it's feminine... it's maternal): "Off with their heads!" She delivers a cruel verdict without an authentic trial, without a crime: very Kafkaesque, very familiar to the three of us friends at lunch due to the politics of each of our geographies.

I wonder about Darya as Latifa is speaking, with a great deal of pain in her eyes: Will I allow my daughter to be erotic? Will I allow her to be seductive? Will I let her dance without saying, she's not really very good, she's just pretending?

Dana, the political activist, says: "Can we get back to what we were talking about before?" She has sons, so she experiences this whole story quite differently. Perhaps after all it is true what Freud says: that anatomy is destiny...[10] Dana probably finds our conversation banal...

So she changes the subject: "Don't you two think that difference is being eliminated in all areas of our contemporary lives, except when it comes to social class?"

Difference within the realms of sex, gender, race, oh, and certainly the idea of generational difference is being taken away, we are all too democratic for such old-school concepts, but my dear, this is a ploy of capitalism: we get rid of all other differences as a cover-up for what clearly, univocally, and without a doubt exists, which is the difference between the poor and the rich. So, essentially, we eliminate all categories of difference, creating empty/dead subjects, yet capitalism offers the cure for that very deadness it creates. If only you can get your hands on that specific object you have been led to believe you want, then magically you will become fully alive, just for a short time, until you need your next fix: a state of mind very similar to the one experienced by the addict.

Latifa intervenes, because we know our friend well enough to know that when she gets into this kind of political discourse, we should intervene:

> I agree with you that the politically correct is the secret weapon of capitalism. Like what is happening with the narrative around sexuality. Which is the death of desire, it is as if we have to take sexuality out of everything—sexuality is associated only with dangers, predators, and diseases.

I say I know a ninety-five-year-old retired psychoanalyst who said to me recently: "Listen, all this sexual stuff does not concern me anymore, that ship has sailed, but boy, I wouldn't want to be a teenage boy in today's climate."

You know, the other day a seven-year-old daughter of a friend looked at an advertisement in the street and said: "Mommy, why is that man wearing make-up and women's clothes and high heels?"

Dana went on:

> Please tell me that your friend did not say a stupid, mortifying thing to her daughter, like "Oh, yes dear, this is freedom, anybody can wear whatever they like, make-up and skirts are not just for women"; please don't confuse this little girl in the name of freedom; freedom comes from accepting limitations, not from unlimited choices.

I suggest that this discourse is intensely nuanced and complicated, that maybe we should leave it for another lunch.

Dana interrupts me, saying: "Why are you two always bringing my interesting political discourses down to a very parochial level of just talking about your kids?"

Trying to please my friend, I say: You know, Adam Phillips says that the psychoanalytic theory of sexual perversion is the story of consumer capitalism. Basically, in sexual perversions your attention is fixated on that one thing that you believe you want, you believe that is the only thing that can satisfy you and your whole focus and attention is spent on getting that. It's just the way consumer capitalism works: you have to get that product, that specific product that you have been led to believe you want, and nothing else will do.[11]

Do we really know what we want in the first place? But Phillips goes further than that, saying life could not be just about "wanting." Intriguing, no? Whether we agree with him or not.

So this wanting limits all your other options and opportunities for satisfaction, attention, and pleasure. He has this beautiful phrase: "tyranny of purpose," in other words, the tyranny of thinking that we really know what we want.

Phillips has this delightful example of distinguishing between taking a three-year-old child for a walk or going for a walk with a three-year-old child. In the former case you have a purpose, taking the child to the park or the shops, but in the latter, the child will just go round in circles: you will not make it more than a few meters forward.

The child is still not a slave to the tyranny of purpose, so they have relatively unmediated powers of attention. You will think that the child is not doing anything, but they are very intensely doing something, it is just unformulated. Phillips goes on to elaborate that we feel we are not going anywhere, whereas the child is going exactly where they want to go.

I feel as if we have somehow landed back in the territory of children, and my friend does not look so pleased. She probably thinks this is the tyranny of children: they become like a sexual perversion of their own for parents. Parents become fixated on their children, and focus all their attention on their offspring. They begin to endlessly send pictures of them to their friends, assuming that they will be interested.

I remember I asked a colleague once when the book that she was working on would be published, and she said: "Not for a while, as for now my libido is otherwise preoccupied with my toddler's bowel movements." Fetishistic indeed, I thought to myself, and I now attempt once more to please my friend Dana, and not submit to the tyranny of motherhood.

I say, my dear Dana, I actually wanted to tell you about a fascinating encounter I had with an Islamic philosopher; I am sure it will please you. So I met with him because he wanted to discuss Freud. Now he is probably one of the most famous, if not *the* most famous, Islamic philosopher in the region, so you can imagine that I was more than pleased to meet with him, and surprised by his deep and genuine interest in Freud. First of all, this very famous man, just like the best of students, had written down his very specific questions regarding Freudian metapsychology. I was totally impressed by his knowledge of Freudian theory and the depth of his questions, and we ended up having a mesmerizing discussion, where I learned a great deal from him. At the end of our conversation I could not resist asking him what he thought about the situation in Iran. He said: "I am optimistic." I asked him to say more, and he said:

> Well, first of all, if you really look at all the countries in the region, they are secretly hoping for an Islamic republic; they are at the beginning of the dream, we are at the end of the nightmare. Look what happened in Egypt, for example, or what is happening in Turkey. Iranians now know more than ever that the state needs to be separate from religion, for everyone's sake, and especially for religion's sake. Also, you have seen our university students: the social sciences are booming in this country; someone who works with these students, as you do, I am sure, sees how desirous they are.

I completely agreed with him, adding that the problem is that I also see many from my social class, my absolutely lost social class, and the optimism I derive from working with my students during the day quickly evaporates during evenings spent with other groups within Iranian society.

Dana is excited now; her eyes are shining. "Oh, please go on," she says, and Latifa laughs, saying: "Now Dana is content."

I go on. Our famous Islamic philosopher went on to say:

> You know there are two fundamental problems woven into the fabric of Iranian society at the moment. One is that within various institutions and ministries, there is a clear Mafia structure: power and positions are often distributed according to your connections and whom you know, not on qualifications; this inevitably leads to corruption, decay, and decline. The other significant problem is that of human rights.

Latifa says: "But my beloved native land, Saudi Arabia, is worse than the Islamic Republic of Iran on both fronts."

Dana says: "True, yours is the worst of all three, but our very own Netanyahu can compete on both fronts: on Mafia structures of corruption and on human rights." Dana is completely pro-Palestine, as, she says, are most intellectuals in Israel, especially leftist intellectuals.

I say: So basically we have concluded that Iran is paradise after all, compared to your countries. We all laugh, and I continue: Do you see what I mean when I say we reach conclusions that are completely indigestible?

I say: But let me finish what the intriguing Islamic philosopher had to say: it's along the lines of what we are talking about. He highlighted two achievements of the Iranian revolution: one is the achievement of reasonably good healthcare for all, the second is the elimination of transmission of power via "bloodlines," something that was part and parcel of the monarchy. So I asked him about the very thing he was talking about earlier: transmission of power via Mafia-like connections. Is it not another version of transmission via bloodlines? Like when you give your son an important position in the government? Our philosopher said:

> That is true in a sense, and that was the case also during the Shah's time. It seems to be the curse of our geography, but at least the candidates for presidency are not selected on the basis of bloodlines. Even if it is a façade, that is still an improvement

—once again voicing his various discontents with the current system, but with a thoughtfulness and fairness that one rarely observes in passionate political discussions.

Another thing close to his heart was getting rid of capital punishment. He said,

> We cannot obliterate parts of ourselves, or the parts of our societies that we do not approve of. We have to face our demons, we have to find a way

to be hospitable to them, for this is the only way of being hospitable to different parts of ourselves. But you know, Gohar, change has to be slow, or there will be bloodshed, and that is not worth it. We have done that: people do not want to give blood, they do not want to die in the name of their ideals or for revolutions in Iran anymore, they are interested in life. I believe in construction, integration, and binding.

The three of us, thankfully, are not in complete agreement about what our Islamic philosopher has said, but we all find it thought-provoking.

I go on proudly telling my friends that he had read and appreciated my "Shahrzad Complex" paper, and all along I secretly thought that Latifa's mother's reaction to her dancing, besides being composed of various shades of Oedipus proper, might be more a case of the "Shahrzad" complex.

Notes

1 *Guardian*, "Iran and Iraq: Remember War that Cost More than a Million Lives."
2 *Guardian*, "Iran and Iraq: Remember War that Cost More than a Million Lives."
3 *Guardian*, "Iran and Iraq: Remember War that Cost More than a Million Lives."
4 James, *Fifty Shades of Grey.*
5 James, *Fifty Shades Darker; Fifty Shades Freed.*
6 *Guardian*, "Fifty Shades of Grey is Fastest Adult Novel to Sell One Million Paperbacks."
7 Busch, *Creating a Psychoanalytic Mind.*
8 Rose, *Mothers.*
9 Winnicott, "Hate in the Counter-Transference."
10 Freud, "A Short Account of Psycho-Analysis."
11 Phillips in conversation with Baum, "Politics in the Consulting Room."

Tell Me a Story
Shahrzad "in Analysis" in Contemporary Persia

Our story begins in a land not that far away, in the city of Shahrzad. Once a harmonious and fertile land, it has been ruined by the maddening terror and fatal rage of King Shahriar, who has been betrayed by his wife. The inhabitants are fleeing the city, attempting to save their daughters' lives.

Once upon a time, there lived a king with two lion-hearted sons: Shahriar and Shah Zaman. After the king's death, the two brothers divide the kingdom, and ruled in harmony and peace for twenty years. Then one day a twist of fate leads both brothers to discover the romantic escapades of their queens. A revengeful Shahriar slays his queen and her lover and, convinced that all women are unfaithful, makes a decision: to deflower a virgin every night and kill her the next morning, to make sure that no woman will ever be unfaithful to him again. After three years of this practice, Shahriar asks his Vizier, the king's highest official, to provide him with an "eligible maid." The Vizier has two daughters, Shahrzad and Dunyazad. When Shahrzad hears about this situation from her father, she volunteers for this marriage. Her father tries to dissuade her with a story: a story that doesn't work, as Shahrzad thanks her father, but pursues her own plan.

"The story that doesn't work" marks the very beginning of the culture of narrative and storytelling within *One Thousand and One Nights*. Therefore, the first story is the one told by the father: a father who, despite his powerful political position at the king's court, allows his daughter to decide her own destiny, as he has faith in her subjectivity and her desire.

On the other hand, it is Shahrzad's belief and knowledge that not all men are the same (her father being the example *par excellence*), which comes from her trust in her own integrated sense of self, and leads her, eventually, to success. It is also noteworthy that another reason for Shahrzad's success is the collaboration of her sister; in fact, the two sisters collude to save the "feminine soul." Hence Shahrzad tells her sister, Dunyazad: "When I'm taken to Shahriar's court, I will ask him to call you in for a last farewell. When our marriage is consummated, come forward and ask me to tell you a story."[3]

Shahrzad was a possible precursor of Freud, to borrow Julia Kristeva's phrase, who discerned the secrets of the mind so well that she altered the fate

DOI: 10.4324/9781003269113-6

of a nation and set the feminine soul free.[4] She saves her own life and brings back a sense of creativity, play, magic, and prosperity to her beloved city. How does she do that? By telling stories, and believing in the magic of the words.

After a thousand and one nights of storytelling, Shahrzad, who is now mother to three sons, asks Shahriar to have mercy on her and let her live. At this point, we should remember that Shahrzad did not give birth to a daughter, and that there is no sign of her mother anywhere; we can already begin to see the problematics, which I will develop further a little later, of the transgenerational mutation of women.

To go back to the story: Shahriar embraces Shahrzad and their sons, begs for her forgiveness, and thanks her for having prevented him from further killings; after years of horror and hate, people are finally living a happy life, at least until "Death, this destructor of all pleasures and separator of loved ones, fell upon them."[5]

It is noteworthy that throughout the book, unlike the well-known formula "And they lived happily ever after," we hear Shahrzad saying something along these lines at the end of each story: "…and they lived a most gratifying, happy life until that which destroys pleasures and separates crowds and destroys palaces and spreads cemeteries came on them…"[6] And so ends each story! Shahrzad, Shahriar, and their three sons live a happy life, until death rides in on their feast, letting Shahrzad join the many voices and characters in her colorful inner world of stories.

***

Many scholarly efforts have been made to find the origins and whereabouts of this book, and everyone agrees on its pre-Islamic roots, though there are disputes over its possibly Indian, Persian, or Arabic origins (there are even a few claims that the book might belong to the Greek literary tradition). But the book that we recognize today as the *One Thousand and One Nights* was first translated—from its Persian predecessor, *Hizaar Afsaan* (*Thousand Legends*)—into Arabic in the third or fourth century of the Hijri (Islamic) calendar. From then on, it became a playground for the bards of Islamic states, finding its way to Egypt, where it was given the current manuscript format sometime in the sixteenth century and was later translated to French for the first time in 1712–1714 by Antoine Galland.[7]

It was the version from Egypt, known as the Bulaq script, that was translated into Persian for a Qajar prince and became the very first Persian text of *One Thousand and One Nights*.

***

At first sight, in comparison to literary "masterpieces," the *Nights* seems like an orphan in the territory of giants! But it is exactly because of this orphan status that the *Nights* is able to be the appropriate host for all that has been suppressed by the cultural status quo! It is interesting to consider how the book has been "moralized" from one translation to another; its contents, just like our dreams, have been the victim of censorship time and again: Ali Asghar Hekmat, Minister of Culture under the Pahlavi Dynasty, one of the brightest and most modern ministers of culture in Iran, advised against reading the *Nights* and instead recommended reading the adventures of "Sinbad" who, according to him, could be a great role model of a "hard-working lad" for the youth of the country![8]

That is why the book ended up acting as a magnetic field, one which attracts the very characters and role models that would otherwise be banned or suppressed according to the contemporary *zeitgeist*! It is strange that, two hundred years after the first Persian translation, this situation of suppression is still ongoing… a situation that is not specific to Persia but was also experienced by the famous French author Marcel Proust in the last century. (Proust mentions his family's advice to read the censored version of the *Nights* and confesses that, ignoring this advice, he secretly read the uncensored version.)[9]

It is for all these reasons that the *Nights* became a collection of the many forbidden images that were not allowed to enter and disrupt the major pervasive image presented by more "official" literary works. Perhaps that is the reason why there are so many different versions of the *Nights*! However, all the versions share two common features: they are all part of what Mikhail Bakhtin calls "The Literature of the Carnivalesque," and all versions host characters who are not accepted by the moralistic values of the time.[10] And doesn't this coincide precisely with Freud's exact definition of the mechanism of repression? And so, isn't this book the "work" of the mind against repression?

One Thousand and One Nights is a text that is not actually the work of a literary scholar but was written by many authors, a text that draws on its diverse frames to create the conditions for dialogue, often between people who are usually absent from the social order: those who are regarded as marginalized or improper.

We must be wary of any account of carnival which simplistically considers the phenomenon as an expression of popular resentments. Bakhtin sees the possibility of a "complete withdrawal from the present order" in the carnival. He refers to this celebration of the incomplete as "gay relativity": an attitude in which all the official certainties are relativized, inverted, or parodied. As Samini says,

> One could even go as far as to call the whole of "One Thousand and One Nights" a scene for this happy carnival of subversion. Carnival is the becoming of time outside of time: note that in the "Nights," Shahriar's brother is called Shah Zaman, the King of Time, and the story actually begins from the time that he, the King of Time, leaves the scene.[11]

***

It is no surprise that repression targets female characters the most. Freud has also described this "repression of femininity" as a "remarkable feature in the psychic life of human beings" equally applicable to both sexes.[12] This repressive force finally finds its way even through our carnivalesque nights, and leaves Shahrzad as the last member of a female generation, with three sons but no daughter.

Where has Shahrzad gone? Why has she disappeared from the theatres of a large number of young contemporary Iranian women's minds? Where have all these various archetypes of women who populate the tales of *One Thousand and One Nights*, night after night, disappeared to? If we consider the *Nights* to be a psychic representation of Shahrzad's internal world, we are immediately impressed with the level of psychic integration that she demonstrates. She does not try to convince the king that all women are good and only good in order to save her own life and those of generations of women to come. She attempts to demonstrate that all women are not the same and that women, like men, can have many different parts. This is closer to third-wave feminism in which women are not categorized and identified as all being the same and having the same desires; hence the idea of "one woman at a time," which is of course reminiscent of the psychoanalytical prescription "one case at a time."

Shahrzad narrates, to the king and to us, the stories of good women and bad ones; she tells of extremely castrating woman who wish to humiliate men, but she also has space for and tales of the opposite in her mind.

She tells us of women loving men, women loving women, women who have sex with both men and women... women with lovers who do not want to marry, women rulers, women commandos, women in charge, self-employed businesswomen, women who are erotic and intelligent at the same time... women who do not wish to have children, maternal women... strong, free-spirited women; but Shahrzad also tells us of those who are victims of men, women who are considered only as erotic objects... and she tells us of women who use their erotic power as sorcery to bewitch, to manipulate, castrate, and humiliate... Shahrzad tells us of cunning, envious, and vengeful women.

Throughout the *Nights*, and in the name of carnivalesque literature, we hear about all kinds of women and men.

Shahrzad's tales are being told during the "unofficial" time of night: outside of time, so to speak (another major resemblance to the unconscious) within an "encyclopedic" carnivalesque genre, a genre with the possibility of contradictions in the "margins." Could it be that Shahrzad manages such a liberating tale within the playground of the unconscious because she is in touch with different parts of herself?

Can we go so far as to suggest that *One Thousand and One Nights* is the tale of Shahrzad herself, and the many parts of herself that she is not afraid to know and to integrate into this final carnival of her own? But where, then, has Shahrzad gone? Why did the daughters of Persia lose her as an original character within contemporary Iranian discourse? Was she repressed and resurrected in a disfigured manner? What remains of Shahrzad is a complete exoticization of her as the ultimate erotic oriental figure...

Shahrzad gave birth to three sons but not a daughter. It seems that a metaphoric trans-generational mutation has occurred: even our carnivalesque text of a thousand nights has not been able to bear the birth of Shahrzad's daughters. But this symbolic mutation or disfiguration has exacted a titanic price from contemporary Iran in general, and its daughters specifically...

Through a psychoanalytical textual interpretation of the *Nights*, I have attempted to uncover the long-lost image of Shahrzad, an eminent female figure whose voice once echoed as a powerful archetype of the Persian woman, a voice which seems to have become fainter throughout the ages.

I have tried to reveal various archetypes of women from the *Nights* that have become completely extinct within a mainstream Iranian discourse. This elimination appears even more powerfully within the clichéd orientalist discourse, in which Iranian women are portrayed, both nationally and internationally, as nothing but the historical victims of a patriarchal and political trajectory... It is tragic to realize that the archetypes of Persian woman who populate the tales of Shahrzad, night after night, have been lost as sources of female identification.

It seems that this transgenerational mutation of Shahrzad's daughters has left the contemporary Iranian discourse regarding women with two choices: either a politicized and victimized trajectory, or to be the new Shahrzad, now become solely an erotic and oriental figure. When we portray victimized women in Iran we are choosing a reductionist view which ignores a large number of working women, women who have been the face of political resistance in the last few decades, women who have taken care of their families upon immigration, women who have refused to submit to the oppressing laws against them, young women who are mostly university educated; with this reductionist view, we are also failing to take into consideration that within the dynamics of some Iranian families, we find castrating women, and hence castrated men.

It is my assertion that this has led to a particular elaboration of the Oedipus complex for women in Iran. As clinical experience has shown me through my practice in Iran over the last twelve years, it seems that for many Iranian girls the object of desire remains the mother (as opposed to the classic Oedipus complex, in which at one point part of the girl's libido is decathected from the mother and attached to her father), which brings up homosexual anxieties that are expressed in a defensive reaction-formation. This can lead to a great deal of destructivity in the psychic representations of envy within what might be called a culture of the Freudian death drive. This, I believe, can have the most dangerous effects upon women and their ability to become creative, playful autonomous subjects.

As Kristeva reminds us, this too seems to be a universal phenomenon, but my clinical observation shows me that it is particularly prominent within the problematics of women's relationships in Iran. Hence to ignore it is to close off any possibility of loving between women.[13]

Kristeva's analysis suggests that we need not only a new discourse of maternity but also a new discourse of the relation between mothers and daughters, a discourse that does not prohibit the love between women through which female subjectivity is actually born.

I have observed, within clinical practice, that too intense a fusional and dyadic relationship seems to be passed on from one generation of women to the next in Iran. We can use the Shahrzad metaphor to say that we were not able to carry out her legacy: she did not give birth to daughters, and so she was not able to pass on her subjective, separated, integrated, and passionate self...

For years we have observed this mutation, this repression of giving birth to a daughter; while having the capacity to let her go, and to teach her the possibilities of loving within a more classical triangulation of our Freudian "family romance." Perhaps the reason that we do not hear about Shahrzad's mother and daughters is that they are within her, one and the same as each other. They are under each other's skin, so to speak, in both senses of the expression in English. They have fallen into her ego; are incorporated within her, encapsulated in the formula of "one body, two minds."

Here I am referring to the English expression "you get under my skin," or "I've got you under my skin." This, interestingly, is an expression both of sexual attraction and of becoming annoyed and angry at someone. Maybe when we are imprisoned in each other's skins there is no escaping the death drive. I may attempt to kill you in order to free myself from you, but what a futile attempt that is, for if "the shadow of the object has fallen upon the ego," as Freud magnificently elaborated in "Mourning and Melancholia" (1917), our unconscious homicidal wishes become nothing more than the suicide of the subject.[14]

Generations of Iranian women experienced a fusional relationship with their mothers, as did their mothers with their own mothers. I wonder if the daughters of Persia are destined to repeat this destiny, one that is not so dissimilar to that of Amazonian women. Or will we try to elaborate on this, and thus allow a third to come in between transgenerations of women? What needs to be stressed here is not the women's genealogy: that is already too durable an adhesive; we need to let men in! (Clearly, I am not talking about an actual man or father but a function, a sort of triangulation, a thirdness; a paternal function that is bound to be introduced only via the desire of the mother.) We need to elaborate on the homosexual/incestuous unconscious wishes and anxieties that inevitably accompany this kind of fusion between mothers and their daughters. Clearly, these issues are nuanced, multilayered, and on a spectrum.

Clinically, I have been astonished at the lack of desire for fathers on the part of a large number of my female analytic patients. The object of desire very often remains the phallic mother. As such, these incestuous feelings on the one hand, and the wish for and fear of separation on the other, are bound to be aroused, and they are uncomfortable and scary: defenses are raised against them. As a reaction formation we see a territory of death, war, and destructiveness emerging between women: a territory of revenge, hate, aggression, and envy. On the surface, and at first glance, this seems indeed to be a discourse of our classic Oedipus, and those dynamics are certainly present, yet upon looking closer, I begin to notice something about these interpretations with regard to aggression: "So, it seems that you have the idea that your mother is mean to you because she wants your father all to herself," did not work as well as "Perhaps your mother wants you all to herself." These libidinal interpretations suddenly opened up the separation/individuation discourse, which, I found, was crucial for those analysands on the road towards integration.

Certainly, there is a whole set of problems for men and boys that one could elaborate from this discourse, but this is for a different essay. However, just to briefly refer to some findings of that paper, how can these castrated passive men, who were babied by their own phallic mother goddesses, unacknowledged by their wives, and therefore by their own children, function as a third? That seems an unlikely outcome. Instead, this could lead to a deliberate vengeful passivity on their part: a sort of active passivity, for example in choosing addictions and bankruptcies, or an even more active choice to act out their unbound aggressions and frustrations in a manner which is faithful, yet again, to the death drive.

This is not a discourse of blame; this is not a moralistic discourse. This is only a precarious desire of mine to attempt to elaborate a few layers of these very complicated and multifaceted Oedipal constellations, hoping to bring new possibilities of psychic integration to the fore.

**

To return to what I have termed the "Shahrzad complex": could this be a rebellion against the law of the father in a society that has patriarchal laws? Perhaps, but the "Shahrzad complex" is the result of the failure of that rebellion, as it has landed on the death drive. Within this complex, the mothers do not seem to have much desire beyond their children. No real thirdness can see the light of day; certainly, I am not discussing a full foreclosure of thirdness, as in psychosis, but within a continuum and relative discourse, in an in-between stage that Gregorio Kohon has brilliantly referred to as the "hysterical stage."

It is impossible not to take a position in relation to the desire of the mother, not to decide who (what sexual being) we are for her. First, we desperately need to believe that we are the object of her desire, and then we have to go through the disillusion and the painful realization that we are not it. This moving away from the primary object is overdetermined, not free. [...]

I would suggest that in the development of the oedipal drama of the woman there is a hysterical stage, in which the subject—caught up in her need to change the object from mother to father—can get "fixed," unable to make the necessary choice. If it were true—as Freud suspected—that a woman will choose a husband according to the image of her father (but establish with him in phantasy the same relationship that she had with her mother), then a woman would always, at heart, remain marked by this hysterical stage. This is not unknown to psychoanalysts in their practices: a female patient might say that she is in love with her male analyst but nevertheless make a maternal transference to him, "and one that is often fiercely denied and frequently has delusional undertones."[15]

I repeat, as I have always said: I do believe in the universality of the Oedipus complex. This is just a slight twist, just a single story describing what I believe is a variation on the Freudian family romance—not in a culturally relativist way, but merely in the sense of different versions of the same story, with all its twists and turns, as we work together with our patients to thicken the plot... .

In the final analysis, carnivalesque literature is the closest one gets to the unconscious and hence *One Thousand and One Nights*, representing a superb example of this genre, becomes an ideal text to search and re-search for what has been lost in the more mainstream Iranian literature and consciousness.

We need to go back to Shahrzad and find space within ourselves to tolerate the birth of her daughters, to resurrect different parts of ourselves that we were unable to face, that we were too afraid to find a tale for: even in the *Nights*, and even inside the carnival of Shahrzad's tales. Let us re-find Shahrzad, the integrated self of Shahrzad, in order to resurrect her daughters.

This piece is a story; in this story we are in search of Shahrzad: the one who could become the object of identification for Iranian women, hoping that re-finding her might lead to a new elaboration of Iranian women's Oedipal complex.

Let us finish at the moment when Shahrzad speaks for the first and last time, on the 978th night. It is the only time she speaks not with a story, but outside of a tale.

> My lord, ... And whoever thinks that all women are the same, falls away from wisdom and his insanity is incurable.[16]

Notes

1 Kristeva, *Tales of Love.*
2 Lane, *The Arabian Nights.*

3 Lane, *The Arabian Nights.*
4 Kristeva, *Tales of Love.*
5 Lane, *The Arabian Nights.*
6 Lane, *The Arabian Nights.*
7 Hekmat, "Moghadame Bar Hezar va Yek Shab (Introduction To A Thousand Nights and One Night)."
8 Hekmat, "Moghadame Bar Hezar va Yek Shab (Introduction To A Thousand Nights and One Night)."
9 Pouillon et al., *Dictionnaire Des Orientalistes de Langue Française.*
10 Bakhtin, *Speech Genres and Other Late Essays.*
11 Samini, "Narration of Violence or Violence of Narration."
12 Freud, "Analysis Terminable and Interminable."
13 Kristeva, *Tales of Love.*
14 Freud et al., *On Murder, Mourning and Melancholia.*
15 Green, cited in Kohon, *No Lost Certainties to Be Recovered*, 207.
16 Lane, *The Arabian Nights*, 2253.

Un-Translation[1]

A few weeks ago, I was having a conversation with my dear friend Lucia, whose mother tongue is Spanish. She and I are both Borges fans; hence we were talking about Borges generally, and his poem "The Other Tiger" specifically. I have used "The Other Tiger" previously in *Doing Psychoanalysis in Tehran* and it is a poem I attempt to return to and rediscover on various occasions.[2] Thirty minutes into our conversation, and a glass of grape juice later, she said: "You can't really understand Borges unless you read him in Spanish, in his primary language, in the language of his mother tongue, in the language of his native land."

I thought: what does "really," and "understand," mean in this context? What was it that Lucia was referring to that cannot be translated? Where is this desirous place that I do not have access to? In short, is she not talking about translation, hospitality, foreignness, paradise and paradise lost, mourning, and separation?

When we fall into the traditional way of working with translation, in which one should read poetry in the language in which it was written, are we not thinking back to the vestiges of our infantile wishes for a paradise, one where we were united in a non-foreign union? Can we say that translation requires the capacity to mourn our paradises lost, where there is no complete understanding of anything? Translation requires a separation, a killing of the mother, of the bliss of our pure fusion. Translation requires letting our fathers in, letting the paternal function in. To access language, we need the capacity for translation.

Of course, there is an un-translatable region of the mind, the part that remains inaccessible. This is the limitation of language, the failure of signifiers; in a sense, it is Lacan's barred subject. We tend to project this un-translatability, which is clearly not a non-translation but an un-translatability. So we say: Only if I could read Borges in Spanish would I be able to avoid this fearful territory of castration, of triangulation, and of the pollution that comes the moment we exit paradise: that pure paradise where there are no signs of parasites, no possibility of mourning and a *club privé* of the melancholic.

DOI: 10.4324/9781003269113-7

Can we elaborate further and say: Let the Farsi-speaking father come into the blissful union of Lucia and her Spanish-speaking mother, and vice versa? Very strange children will be produced, very Calibanesque offspring, foreigners with strange features and accents from far-away geographies, but can we be hospitable to them? Can we be a poetic hospitable host?

As such, can we let Caliban "in"—not because of our humanitarian ambitions, but because we cannot envision a Caliban-less world, that world we find utterly boring, the violent kind of boredom? The boredom of psychosis, of fatherless states, where there are no minor languages, as Mariano Horenstein reminds us.[3]

Caliban is born out of foreignness: is this foreignness not the same foreignness we experience when we are thrown out of the paradise of our blissful union with our mothers, motherlands, and native tongues? The same foreignness of getting to know our unconscious, of getting to know the other, the foreignness of the woman, of this absence within ourselves?

Let us envision a hospitality, for "Hospitality—this is culture itself,"[4] not with the illusion of conquering this un-translatable space of our mind, nor in the vain attempt at complete understanding, and of course not to adhere to cultural relativism, but to grant hospitality:

> This unconditional law of hospitality, if such a thing is thinkable, would then be a law without imperative, without order and without duty. A law without law, in short. For if I practice hospitality "out of duty" [and not only "in conforming with duty"], this hospitality of paying up is no longer an *absolute hospitality*, it is no longer *graciously offered beyond debt and economy offered to the other*, a hospitality invented for the singularity of the new arrival, of the unexpected visitor.[5] (my emphasis)

Lucia said that there was something missing, but why is it that we forget that it is precisely because of that missing thing that we have minds? If it were not for that absence, we would not be able to think and to play, so I invite you, in the name of hospitality, to host a few lines of the un-translation into Farsi of Borges' poem in my words:

بورخس از ببر نماد ها می گوید؛

ببر نماد ها که در برابرش ببر واقعی را قرار می دهد

این یکی از دیدن کله ی گاومیش ها خونش به جوش می آید

اما با نامی بر او نهادن، که همانا تلاشی است برای کوچک کردن دنیایش

او نیز ببری خیالی می شود که دیگر زمین و زمان را زیر پا نمی گذارد

Lucia, the patron saint of the blind, live up to the signifier of your name, my friend, and let us adhere to Borges' blindness and the "seeing" that accompanies this non-seeing. This representation which comes specifically from the submission to the un-translatable, the un-representable. This finding through absence that comes from a non-puritan triangulation, where we develop the possibility of the mind, where we can be hospitable to the nameless foreigner, to the "un-expected visitor" in the "Other Tiger." Lucia, let us mourn together, let us play together in this territory of absence, in the realm of the pleasure principle, offering a Derridean poetic, one which is hospitable to foreignness just because she has read Borges in Farsi; the one found in verse.

Notes

1 This chapter is adapted with permission from an article in *Calibán*: Gohar Homayounpour (2015), "Un-Translation." *Calibán, Latin-American Journal of Psychoanalysis*, 13 (1), 140–142.
2 Homayounpour, *Doing Psychoanalysis in Tehran.*
3 Horenstein, *The Compass and the Couch.*
4 Cixous and Derrida, *Veils*, 361.
5 Derrida, "Hostipitality," 83.

Caliban

Across various discourses of otherness, the sole focus is on the relationship between Prospero and Caliban, a relationship which is indeed essential.

But what if one attempts to escape such a binary approach and to dream that Shakespeare's play had a twist, and another Caliban showed up? Caliban in relation to Caliban: is this not a new "in-between" space to be explored? Is it not impregnated with infinite possibilities of fantasies and transformations? Of new paradigms on how to be with the other?

I have been thinking about this idea for a long time; the image of "what happens when Caliban meets an(O)ther Caliban?" When I was invited to go to New Delhi with twenty of our students from the Freudian Group of Tehran, I considered this Indo-Iranian encounter to be a meeting of this sort, of two Calibans. I wanted to finally explore this new encounter and the exceptional opportunity it offered us. I wanted to see how my thoughts transformed in this particular geographical scene.

Prospero's shadow will inevitably accompany our two Calibans, but their own relationship in this new formulation/triangulation that gives space to an (O)ther Caliban could be thrilling to explore. Within this dream, new identities, friendships, and characters will emerge. Prospero's identity will inevitably be transformed, along with those of our two Calibans.

In my image, in my dream, this new relationship transforms the master–slave dialectic into a subversive psychoanalytic discourse of difference and unfamiliarity. Envisioning a politics of re-veiling, of an ultimate game of hide and seek (*Fort/Da*) between our two Calibans, in the playground of monsters. This only becomes possible due to the arrival of an "other" Caliban, as our third. This third, our third, is not a cruel, punitive and sadistic paternal function, but one that has not silenced its passivity or femininity. Instead, our "unexpected visitor," our "other" Caliban, attempts to play with the Sycorax within throughout this de-territorializing process and across this narrative of a "tale of tales."

The Tempest is believed to have been Shakespeare's last play. This particular play has created a great deal of interest within various discourses on otherness over the years, featuring especially within colonial and postcolonial critiques.

DOI: 10.4324/9781003269113-8

In this play, Caliban plays the role of the monster/servant of Prospero. His mother is Sycorax, a powerful witch banished from Algiers for sorcery "so strong / that [she] could control the Moon."[1] Sycorax arrives already pregnant with Caliban, and dies immediately after his birth, before Prospero's takeover of the island.

A simple Google search enlightens us on yet another binary approach to the Caliban–Prospero relationship: it is also read as a typical colonial master–slave dynamic, with Prospero representing all that is evil about the colonizer and Caliban the Caliban/cannibal, the definition of stranger: non-integrated, non-assimilated, the different one; "*l'inconnu*," an alternative word for stranger from French: the unknown. In short, he is the ultimate victim and abused slave of Prospero.

However as psychoanalysts we know better than this: the relationship between master and slave is much more nuanced. Following Hegel's dialectic, the philosopher Robert Brandom explains:

> Hegel's discussion of the dialectic of the Master and Slave is an attempt to show that asymmetric recognitive relations are metaphysically defective… Asymmetric recognition in this way is authority without responsibility, on the side of the Master, and responsibility without authority, on the side of the Slave. And Hegel's argument is that unless authority and responsibility are commensurate and reciprocal, no actual normative statuses are instituted.

Another frequent interpretation offered for the Caliban–Prospero relationship is the eroticization of Caliban, which is very much a parallel for the manner in which I believe Iran/Islam to have been viewed as the new modern erotic: a phenomenon which I have previously termed Islamo-fetisho-phobia. I think this is precisely part of the problematic of today's socio-politico-culture in Iran.[2]

Thus, as Carlos Padrón tells us in his "Discussion on Psychoanalysis in Minor Language" with Mariano Horenstein at IPTAR:[3]

> The Center exoticizes the Margins (as happened with "Magical Realism," once it became mainstream, or as happened, and continues to happen in Europe, in considering the so-called New World as the haven or paradise of the *bon sauvage*, where the Margins become an object of desire for the Center because it contains the magical reverse of what the Center does not have and thus craves for: an enigmatic and sexy secret…

In the struggle between the master and the slave for recognition (the struggle to be recognized by the other), the master might exoticize (make more desirable or idealize) the slave so as to experience, to its maximum, the recognition by the slave's (the margin's) desire, once it happens. Yet the opposite effect might also occur: the slave (the margin) might self-exoticize himself so as to receive the maximum amount of gratification once he is recognized by the master's (the center's) desire.

These are precisely the problematics of Iran today, in its appointed role as the modern erotic Caliban chosen by Prospero. A vivid example can be found in what has happened with Iranian art in the past two decades or so: one gets the feeling that not many subversive works are being produced. Especially within the domain of visual arts, a wide array of Persian delights are put together and sold at very high prices in Prospero's market, without a critical gaze.

A very different phenomenon happened within Iranian cinema, where I would go as far as to say that following Sohrab Shahid-Saless and Abbas Kiarostami, and the cinematic genre they have created, Iranian cinema has been at its highest level of artistic production, providing brilliant internationally acclaimed movies, especially after the Islamic revolution.

Why has Iranian cinema been able, for the most part, to produce masterpieces, while in art we have predominantly moved further and further into a bizarre territory of mediocrity? This would be an interesting question to explore further, and furthermore I am not, of course, idealizing all of our cinema and banalizing Iranian art in general. This is merely an observation which attempts to elaborate on the dangers of producing Persian erotic delights.

Could this be an unconscious pact made between Prospero and Caliban in order to escape darkness, difference and the unknown? There are clear neurotic gains for both of our fallen heroes. No matter how faithfully this pact will maintain the status quo, they will miss out on the magnificent monstrous tales of the island, of themselves, and of the other. They will never know the joys and laments of playing together, truly knowing each other, and above all of having the exhilarating privilege of encountering their unconscious.

The two options mentioned above are in a sense two sides of the same coin, with both parties incarcerated in a dyadic prison of sameness and not of difference: as psychoanalysts, we are indeed familiar with the menace of dyadic prisons.

Here in my vision, our third is an unexpected visitor, another Caliban. What if the play had a twist: an "other" act, so to speak?

Well, there is a danger that one Caliban would feel superior to the other, reproducing the asymmetrical relationship between Prospero and Caliban, which is what has often happened in former colonies.

This could become part of the problematics of our two Calibans' engagement. Here the passive participant in the Caliban–Prospero relationship turns into an active one to master the trauma. The master remains quite powerful within these re-enactments.

Hence, one Caliban evaluates his degree of Prospero-ness in comparison with the other Caliban. Here Prospero has been internalized as Caliban's ego ideal; this is what our two Calibans need to work through, this is where Prospero's imaginary powers come from. Prospero is Caliban's superego, a superego in which, as Slavoj Žižek tells us, the more one obeys, the guiltier one becomes. Maybe this is what needs to happen in the Indo–Iranian encounter: we need to do superego work; maybe this can happen only in a meeting of Calibans. Can we envision a Caliban free from this ego ideal, or even playing with Prospero's ideas of himself? Isn't this what psychoanalysis should represent? Caliban says: "You, the 'Other,' imprison me in this image; well, I will go further, I will give you a hyperreal image, let's play."

I have a proposal: our two Calibans could play a game of hide and seek in the playground of monsters.

In this in-between space we might be able to find Caliban "Subjects" who are not angry with Prospero, who are not submissive to his discourse; they just think he is really funny. Isn't the superego comical, after all?

Often with the arrival of "the third" we are to tolerate a cruel, sadistic, punitive paternal function. Often with our symbolic fathers there is a rejection of femininity, of passivity; that of castration. They reject the all-powerful witch and her terrifying magic. Shakespeare, within the theatre of his mind in *The Tempest*, silences Sycorax from the very start, Caliban's mother, whose etymology represents a pig and a crow. Is this not the same terror and angst of both genders that made the father of psychoanalysis bow to the powers of the underworld, of the unconscious, in "Analysis Terminable and Interminable"?[4]

In order to move away from the binary master–slave dialectic we need a calibanesque analyst's discourse, one that is consciously a subversion of the master discourse, of the mainstream language of Prospero's book.

This father has to not only not have silenced Sycorax but to have heard her dreamlike stories; Sycorax is Shahrzad of the *One Thousand and One Nights*; this sorcerer is the one who saves us from the "beyond the pleasure principle" because he/she has a feminine voice, because the language of narratives and storytelling is feminine, magical, brutal. Hence our third Caliban is the name of the father that is Caliban, and yet this father is also a feminine arrival, one who has heard the feminine voice within "himself."

Here we are very close to Kristeva's imaginary father, a concept she develops out of Freud's "father in individual prehistory." This father is a combination of mother and father, a "mother–father conglomerate."[5] It has no sex difference, but the choice of both feminine and masculine; it can have both faces: that of a loving father and the stern Oedipal father.

In this proposed politics we move from a dialectic to a trialectic, that is, the road out of nightmares (failed dreams) to dreams, creativity, and transformations. Traveling upon this road becomes possible only with the entrance of our fathers, but they have to be familiar with the Sycorax within, to have heard her, to have loved her, to have feared her, and to have encountered her: in short, to have been hospitable to her.

We could enjoy a carnival of masks of Calibans, of "Caliban(a)s": this is a community of subjects hospitable toward themselves and the other, the other within themselves in the name of a politics of unfamiliarity, of ambiguity, and of becomings.

Let us play hide and seek with our Caliban neighbor, because it is only through the darkness in hiding that we can find our Caliban third. He will not reveal himself in daylight, only in an in-between space. We have to make an effort to find him.

I propose a politics of re-veiling, which could be "revealing" after all, with respect to this magical space of "in-betweenness," in this space between hiding and revealing, at that very moment when the curtain is going up, within the very act of revealing where we are inevitably hiding.

But this universal right of hiding/revealing, this Freudian game of *Fort/Da* (hide and seek, *cache-cache*) is being taken away from us in this corrupt culture of the primacy of transparency, as Gerard Wacjman tells us, where nothing is supposedly left to be revealed.[6] No space is left for secrets. Societies must be transparent in order to be legitimate; but psychoanalysis can be legitimate only if it is veiled.

Our existence is related to the ability of hiding, for it is in this territory between the veiling and unveiling that we develop the ability to think.

We want to know what is behind the curtain, what is going on in our parents' bedroom, which for Freud is the seed for the desire for knowledge. So with un-veilings we are killing desire and the ability for this triangulation that is ultimately to *know* as opposed to *see*. If we see everything, what is left to know, to try to find out?

Desire is possible as long as we have not unveiled the last veil: these doors cannot be completely opened as long as you speak in this in-between space, in this space of desire, for as soon as we open the doors, we are in this territory of *jouissance*. If we remove the last veil, we say farewell to any possibilities of passion and intimacy... we could join in this politics of re-veiling because we do not have the illusion of truth-finding, of lights and familiarities, but the liberating knowledge that there is nothing behind the curtain, only that which was left there by us, and no amount of unveiling will unveil the truth that is not there.

Let me very briefly apply this politics of difference and not that of sameness, in the name of our newly arrived Caliban, to a few areas of our contemporary discourse. Allow me to give you just these fleeting examples, which do not do justice to the complicated notions mentioned, but I think they do give a feel of what I wish to communicate.

Immigration

Once upon a time, a patient eloquently elaborated: "Do you know why I terminated my analysis with my American analyst? Because she was adamant about doing extensive research on the Iranian culture right after we met, to find out everything about 'me' and my culture." This is the *zeitgeist* of transparency.

> I had to come to an Iranian analyst with whom I would not automatically be named the "Iranian immigrant" patient. With you I can rest assured that I will not be named, and categorized. Your familiarity, paradoxically, allows an unfamiliarity that I was not granted by my previous analyst. I am hoping you will not claim to know my Iranian culture.

Trauma

The contemporary politics of trauma, especially the literature on refugees, highlights the point I am trying to bring to light. Where the ideas of victimhood and trauma are forced upon all "refugees" on arrival, all the other possibilities of translation are forbidden. It is as if we have a script ready to hand to them, and they must learn to play the role, rather like "method acting," becoming the sole character they are intended to play. Do we not become the traumatizer, when we forcefully put them into this named, already neatly prepared, category of a traumatized person, whom we can only heal now we have categorized them? Do we not in the process concretize our own sense of identity, away from all the possibilities of symbolic representation in the territory of the imaginary? Do we not become the aggressor at the very moment when we claim to be at our most humanitarian? Of course, the healer and the traumatized person are both sides of the same coin, and for both the possibility of becomings is taken away.

But it is only through this proposal of re-veiling that we can allow this unfamiliarity.

Freud asserts, in *The Interpretation of Dreams*: "Until now you had hoped that I was going to deliver you to light, but we are moving more and more into darkness."[7] Incidentally, another meaning of Caliban is darkness, blackness, and obscurity.

My image, my dream, and psychoanalysis are, I believe, possible only within a politics of darkness—in a "psychoanalysis to come," as the Argentine psychoanalyst Mariano Horenstein puts it.[8]

I want to join the Carnival of Calibans, especially in geographical territories that the IPA (International Psychoanalytic Association) used to call "the rest of the world"; in awakening the spirits of the underworld, of the unconscious, toward a discourse of desire narrated within and beyond one thousand and one tales.

Notes

1 Shakespeare, *The Tempest*, 262.
2 Brandom, Interview with Robert Brandom on "Making It Explicit" Part 1.

3 Horenstein, "Psychoanalysis in Minor Language with Mariano Horenstein at IPTAR—Archive."
4 Freud, "Analysis Terminable and Interminable (1937)."
5 Kristeva, *Black Sun.*
6 FRAC Lorraine, "L'intime Exposé, L'intime Extorqué."
7 Freud, *The Interpretation of Dreams.*
8 Horenstein, *The Compass and the Couch.*

One Should Build a Boat

E, a really big and muscular man from Azerbaijan, suffers from severe anxiety, usually related to something catastrophic happening. He will get cancer, or his wife will have an accident, or his son will catch the flu and won't be able to breathe, or, if they manage to miraculously survive all such imminent risks, then we will surely all be doomed by the very obvious earthquake that is certain to shake Tehran and all its inhabitants. E has done his research impeccably, and I am bound to tell you that, in reality, Tehran is indeed in danger of earthquakes to come. Yet, as the beginning of my favorite and probably most oft-used interpretation goes: "I hear what you are saying, but putting reality aside for a moment..." In any case, E has his earthquake bag ready at all times.

One day, in his usual thick Turkish accent, he associates anxiously on the couch. It's right after his car has been broken into and stolen.

> Doctor, you can see why I feel anxious all the time, for as hard as I try to keep the people I love safe, to keep my home, my car safe, there is nothing I can do... I feel impotent... I cannot stop thinking about the thief and what he is doing to the body of my car, how he is probably pulling it apart piece by piece to sell as we speak. I feel such violent, sadistic fantasies towards him... you know, I had all kinds of alarms and everything... you see, I am completely impotent...

E goes on:

> When we were young kids, my sister, my brother and I would travel to the Caspian Sea, where we would build sandcastles on the vast beaches. I would do everything to protect my sandcastles from the waves destroying them, building my sandcastles further and further from the sea, but still a really high wave would come in and destroy it. Maybe my sandcastle would be safe for hours, or even a day or so, but eventually I would have to face the fact that my sandcastle was taken over by the sea. You cannot imagine how I would spend hours strategizing to protect my sandcastle,

DOI: 10.4324/9781003269113-9

adding wood and blocks, using certain newly imagined architectural tricks... but alas! The sea, the waves would always defeat me... why were my sandcastles all destroyed, no matter how hard I tried?

At this point I merely highlight his last statement, with an emphasis on the "*my*"...

Why were *my* sandcastles all destroyed, no matter how hard I tried?

I was struck by the image of a young boy desperately trying to save his very transient sandcastle, while appreciating the image of the creativity of that young boy, playing architect, attempting to be the architect of himself and his life.

He laughs at my highlighting his statement. By now he knows his analyst well enough to know that I am highlighting his narcissism, his grandiosity... he knows that if he takes more than a few minutes to acknowledge it, I will go for it. He knows that I will say: Do you think anybody's sandcastles have ever survived? Anywhere in the world, on any beach? How grandiose of you to think only your sandcastles were not able to resist their natural destiny... Sandcastles are made to be taken over by the sea, they are by nature transient, and it is this very transience that makes them memorable.

I also know E well enough by now to have some thoughts about his associations. I know that while in the scene that he was describing he still had not lost his father to lethal cancer, he went on to watch his well-built, six-foot-four father lose almost all his weight in six months, becoming fragile right before his eyes, at the precise moment when my patient was in the midst of a ripe Oedipal struggle. How terrifying it must have been for him to watch their world turn upside down. E's father was an amazing father to his kids, and when he died the family really felt their whole lives crumble; they fell apart just like a sandcastle.

Yes, in the above scene his father was still alive, but this is indeed one of the most important concepts in psychoanalysis: that of *Nachträglichkeit* or *après-coup*: a concept which, according to Freud, defines trauma, and particularly the afterward interpretation and idiosyncratic translation made by each individual of ambiguous events, or in Adam Phillips' words, reprints of memory "in accordance with later experience."[2] Freud points to this idea early on when he writes: "a memory is repressed which has only become a trauma by deferred action."[3] Elsewhere, Lacan elaborates that it is the translation by "others" which determines the traumatic effect of an event.[4]

Sergio Benvenuto encapsulates this fundamental concept in psychoanalysis with a fictional clinical example that finds an "embodiment" in Mr. E:

Let us imagine a connection of this type. A subject crosses a bridge. Then he reads that the area has a high seismic risk and that years earlier that same bridge had collapsed, but the information does not particularly trouble him. Years later he sees a house collapse because of an earthquake, and later he develops a phobia for bridges. He can no longer cross them for fear that they will collapse. It's an imaginary clinical case, but a plausible one. What happens here? Let's leave out any symbolic interpretations of the phobia. What counts is that the first experience of crossing the bridge only becomes the cause of a phobia through the sense that the later event gives to the former: collapsing. A previous Event I becomes a cause, thanks to a sense given après-coup by Event II.

Indeed, the concept of après-coup is fundamental precisely because that of which après-coup is an "after" which refers back to a "before" that remains suspended, an x, an unknown element. The paradox of après-coup is that at the beginning there is an after, never a primacy. It is an after often without a before. It does not lead us to the primacy of the other, but at the "primacy of the after."[5]

To return to the by-now infamous scene at the beach where E desperately, anxiously, and in vain tries to protect his transient sandcastles: there have already been many "before" events that trembled his metaphoric castles: such as, for example, the revolution in Iran when his mother was imprisoned for some time, and the births of his siblings, but it is not until years "after," during the tragic and slow decomposition of his strong father right before his eyes, that the collapse of the sandcastles begins to be translated into a traumatic scene based on his dangerous and lethal omnipotence: a scene from his primary narcissism, where we all begin and where all of our libidinal energy is cathected to our own egos. The sandcastle scene/dream becomes a traumatic scene only *après-coup*.

It is not only our past that shapes our future, it is via the future that we translate the past; this is the primacy of the after discussed above by Benvenuto.

E and I have spent many analytic hours talking about how guilty he must have felt when his Oedipal wish to kill his father in order to be with his mother came true. How powerful, even omnipotent, how scared of his own impulses he must have felt; how dangerous he was! He wished for it and it happened (which is indeed a belief reminiscent of the days of our primary narcissism, of magical thinking), especially because he was left now with two incestuous objects—his sister, his mother—and also with his very fragile younger brother (who had been a substitute Oedipal figure before his father died). How dangerous everything must have felt! And so he turns it all into anxiety; he spends years after the death of his father unconsciously paralyzing himself completely; at the moment when he started analysis he was unsuccessful, and defeated at everything in life, but safe, and the ones he loved were safe from his impulses, both sexual and aggressive.

When he describes the thief that day in his session, I cannot but hear an identification with the thief: he always feels as if he stole something from his father, within his imagined Oedipal triumph.

The "body" of the car chimed with the body of the father, taken apart by the cruel cancer, by the forbidden wishes of the thieving son.

But there is also an identification with the car, an identification with the body of the car, the cancer-ridden body of the father, the sandcastle falling apart abruptly, suddenly, to a point of no return. He often wishes/fears he will get a very similar cancer to his father, as an attempt to stay with his loved father, to deny his loss, to keep making and playing with toy "cars" with him, which was one of his favorite pastimes with his father as a young boy.

Over the years one could hear, across his associations, the remains of a negative Oedipus complex as well, in which he becomes sadistic with women and eroticizes the father and especially the father's body. One day when we were discussing this topic he ironically said: "Why do you call this one the negative Oedipus complex: who decides which one is positive and which one is negative?" I thought that was an excellent point.

Or is the cancer wish/fear also a need for punishment for his classic Oedipal wishes? Oh, if he only knew of the ordinariness of these wishes as well; even here our protagonist is not special, he is an average neurotic, with the most ordinary of Oedipal wishes, and we know that everybody's sandcastles fall apart, even the most extraordinary of sandcastles.

I think of a touching little paper by Freud, "On Transience," in which he elaborates on two friends' inability to enjoy the beauty of the smiling, sunny countryside while they stroll together on such a lovely summer day, as they cannot help but anticipate the natural doom of such lovely summer flowers in full bloom upon the arrival of winter.[6]

Freud goes on to say,

> but this demand for immortality is a product of our wishes too unmistakable to lay claim to reality: what is painful may none the less be true. I could not see my way to dispute the transience of all things, nor could I insist upon an exception in favor of what is beautiful and perfect. But I did dispute the pessimistic poet's view that the transience of what is beautiful involves any loss in its worth.

And he goes on to explain the economics of enjoyment: "A flower that blossoms only for a single night does not seem to us on that account less lovely."

As Freud fails to convince his friends with these arguments, he thinks about why he cannot do so, and certainly assumes there must be strong psychological factors at work:

> The idea that all this beauty was transient was giving these two sensitive minds a foretaste of mourning over its decease; and, since the mind

instinctively recoils from anything that is painful, they felt their enjoyment of beauty interfered with by thoughts of its transience.

[...] We possess, as it seems, a certain amount of capacity for love—what we call libido—which in the earliest stages of development is directed towards our own ego. Later, though still at a very early time, this libido is diverted from the ego on to objects, which are thus in a sense taken into our ego. If the objects are destroyed or if they are lost to us, our capacity for love (our libido) is once more liberated; and it can then either take other objects instead or can temporarily return to the ego. But why it is that this detachment of libido from its objects should be such a painful process is a mystery to us and we have not hitherto been able to frame any hypothesis to account for it. We only see that libido clings to its objects and will not renounce those that are lost even when a substitute lies ready to hand. Such then is mourning.

He goes on to refer to all that has been lost after the war, which certainly includes far more horrific losses than the beauty of the countryside:

We cannot be surprised that our libido, thus bereft of so many of its objects, has clung with all the greater intensity to what is left to us, that our love of our country, our affection for those nearest us and our pride in what is common to us have suddenly grown stronger. But have those other possessions, which we have now lost, really ceased to have any worth for us because they have proved so perishable and so unresistant? To many of us this seems to be so, but once more wrongly, in my view. I believe that those who think thus, and seem ready to make a permanent renunciation because what was precious has proved not to be lasting, are simply in a state of mourning for what is Lost. Mourning, as we know, however painful it may be, comes to a spontaneous end. When it has renounced everything that has been lost, then it has consumed itself, and our libido is once more free (in so far as we are still young and active) to replace the lost objects by fresh ones equally or still more precious. It is to be hoped that the same will be true of the losses caused by this war. When once the mourning is over, it will be found that our high opinion of the riches of civilization has lost nothing from our discovery of their fragility. We shall build up again all that war has destroyed, and perhaps on firmer ground and more lastingly than before.

E became anxious as a defense against mourning, as a defense against building a boat to go beyond, in the way that Odysseus did. In mourning, you have to face loss, ambivalence and pain, but there is a possibility of an afterwards. Let us imagine that Odysseus was not able to cross over to the beyond: there would be nothing poetic about our Homeric tragedy. Odysseus had to make a decision between Scylla and Charybdis, and indeed he had to lose and mourn several sailors by choosing Scylla, our six-headed monster, but he made that choice and crossed to the beyond on his boat.

So, by now we have established that there is a timelessness to melancholia and that there exists a primary narcissism, through which you are hyper-cathected with too much libido upon your own ego, in which you have temporarily left the world of objects, to find yourself alone without a boat, without the possibility of a "beyond."

***

As I write these pages, it does not escape me that there is a chain of associations to water; to the blue of the ocean, to naming my daughter Darya (which, as I said above, means the sea in Farsi), to deep-diving and swimming metaphors, to the need to build a boat to go beyond the sea, beautifully encapsulated in the poem "To Come (After)" by Sohrab Sepehri, an undeniably modern Iranian poet.

My father drowned in Lake Leman. Although he was an excellent swimmer, his heart gave in. He was alone that day, his only company a little boat he took to the lake for his afternoon swims. He had a bottle of water, his favorite Swiss chocolate, and an apple with him. He was wearing a blue cotton shirt that we had bought together. When we were growing up, he would always advise my brother and me, and everyone else for that matter, on three things:

Learn English really well, become a good swimmer, and never forget that literature is fundamental to one's life.

H_2O is the chemical formula for water, which consists of two atoms of hydrogen and one atom of oxygen. Swimming could bring us back to the calm, protective waters of the womb...

...it brings out our hidden desires for a return to security and to irresponsibility.

But it also exposes us to the danger of losing our ground, of drifting away...

In the water, we feel ourselves to be in two worlds—one isolated and protective, in which we can be absorbed into fantasy; the other one frightening and dangerous, in which we can take one wrong breath and die. Because of the intersection of these two worlds, swimming is also representative of the oceanic feeling; I find it is a metaphor which encapsulates the wish for and fear of oneness with the world. Here we could die from lack of oxygen, yet here is also one of the most freeing experiences of our lives. We are in proximity to a wished-for security, but able to navigate, finding our own stories taking us to shores unexplored.

I think of the story of the Swiss architect Le Corbusier, who died of a heart attack while swimming, and Arthur Cravan, who was last seen in the water, and disappeared into the liquid element.[7] Such great literature has been written about swimming, such as *Haunts of the Black Masseur: The Swimmer as Hero* by Charles Sprawson.[8]

I read such literature as a means of staying close to my father. It is the rare and poetic souls who die while swimming. The sea and the oceans are not the earth, and are not heaven; they are the site of mystery, the element of mermaids, stories, Atlantis, whales, tides, and treasures. The water surrounds the land, and helps to form the air. If he did not collapse on the ground, but died floating—that means a lot. He is not stuck; he will always exist between two worlds.

***

For some strange reason I am reminded of a summer afternoon in Tehran, when I was a young girl. My father and I were having tea with AK, a dear friend and a paternal figure for me. As we were talking, my father, who at the time was living in Shiraz again (Shiraz was his motherland and where he had spent his paradise years) started telling us, with his usual, affect-laden words, that the other day he had been hard at work on a piece he was writing on Proust in his flat in Shiraz. Noon was approaching and he was getting hungry, and in his usual manner he was wondering where he would order his lunch, when suddenly from the nearby balcony he heard the sweet voice of a woman shouting with the most charming Shiraz accent, across her own balcony to her father's house. "Papa," she said, "our eggplant stew is ready, the table is set, we are about to eat, come over for lunch."

My father continued: "At that moment I thought we definitely must have lived our life the wrong way, you and I, my dear AK. I know you are as much in search of a home-cooked meal as I am." AK replied in complete agreement, shaking his head, full of longing. Both my father and AK were in complete idealization of the life of our eggplant-stew girl's papa. I felt angry at both of them. Not only was I a disappointment to them, due to my lack of ability to cook an eggplant stew, but they were disappointing me: two of the most brilliant men I knew regressing to a primitive state, in which their desire concluded in an eggplant stew.

Today, I think differently. I think the royal road to reasonable psychic health comes via integration. My father and AK were men of high qualities, who might very reasonably wish for a homemade meal, prepared by their daughter. They were intellectual men who could very well wish for a more traditional life than the one they had chosen to live.

I remember a very significant moment in my analysis, when I was complaining passionately about a loved colleague and how betrayed I felt by something she had done. My analyst, my darling Freudian analyst, with his charming New York accent, pressed me on my narcissism, and God bless him for never infantilizing me, for believing I was strong when I did not, and for saying: "You keep talking about loving her, but are you usually this unforgiving of faults in your loved ones?" I will never forget the effect that Dr. J's interpretation/intervention had on me… let me remind the reader that this incident is from my early years of analysis. Rest assured that I have since become a great deal less narcissistic.

I remember too the excitement of that freezing day when my father and I participated together in a demonstration in Montreal against the separation of Quebec from the rest of Canada. He was a firm believer in integration and not separation. His PhD thesis was on the reasons why Azerbaijan should not be separated from Iran. Remarkably, integration becomes a possibility only if we have broken out of our primary narcissism: if, despite our deep desire to turn our daughter into an eggplant-stew kind of girl, we have allowed her to cross the world in search of her own desire. But perhaps the problem is these very binaries. There is an eggplant-stew-maker in all of us, as there is an absence of one in every single one of us.

Binaries are limiting, and the moment that we exclude the possibility of being anything else in our selves, that is when we become an island and start shooting bows and arrows over to the mainland. We must integrate our various parts: the feminine and the masculine, the good and the bad, the eggplant stew and Proust. For the moment that we reject a part of ourselves, we project this to the outside world, and regress to a time when everything good belonged to the inside and everything bad to the outside. And then we are in trouble, in our vain, unreasonable request to keep the part we rejected hidden within ourselves, otherwise known as neurosis. Azerbaijan belongs with Iran—not *to* Iran, but *with* it, as does Iran with Azerbaijan, as does Quebec with Canada and vice versa.

I had a dream last night about my father. In the dream, I can see my father at the height of his youth, wearing his favorite khaki jacket and a particular hat he would often wear. We were at the airport, at a gate. He was the first in line, about to board the plane, and I was a long way behind. I kept calling his name, but he could not hear me. I said Wait for me! and he just got on the plane, never looking back, and the moment he was out of my sight, I woke up.

Beyond Seas

I shall build a boat

I shall build a boat

I shall launch it in the water

I shall sail away from this strange land

Where there is no one in the bush of love

To awaken the heroes.

A boat empty of net

And no longing for pearls in the heart

I will sail my boat and sail some more

Won't lose my heart to the blues

Won't lose it to the sea—nor to the mermaids

Whom in the light of the fishermen's solitude

Spread their lengthy tresses

I shall continue sailing

"One should sail away, sail away."

Beyond the seas there is a town

Where the windows are open to epiphanies

The rooftops are home to pigeons

That look at the effervescence of human intelligence

Where every ten-year-old has a branch of wisdom

The inhabitants look at barricades

As if they were a flame or a sweet dream

The Earth hears the music of your feeling

And the fluttering sound of mythological birds are heard in the wind.

Beyond the seas there is a town

Where the sun is as wide as the eyes of early risers

Poets inherit water, wisdom and light

Beyond the seas there is a town!

One must build a boat

One must build a boat.

Sohrab Sepehri[9]

Notes

1 Freud, "Project for a Scientific Psychology," 281–391.
2 Phillips, *On Flirtation*.
3 Freud, "Project for a Scientific Psychology," 281–391.
4 Lacan and Fink, *Écrits: The First Complete Edition in English*.
5 Benvenuto, "The Après-Coup, Après Coup," 72–87.
6 Freud, "On Transience," 305–307.
7 Biography, "Le Corbusier"; Wikipedia, "Arthur Cravan."
8 Sprawson, *Haunts of the Black Masseur—The Swimmer as Hero*.
9 Sepehri, "Beyond Seas" (my translation).

The Freudian Group of Tehran

Triumphs and Laments

Now, let me seize this moment to briefly tell you about the Freudian Group of Tehran, where we do not have any official registration with the Iranian government, nor are we able to offer our students and candidates any sort of certificates or diplomas, as we are not associated with any Iranian university. Moreover, we are not officially recognized by any international associations.

How come, then, we have about 250 members in Tehran and Mashhad, and a continual and insistent desire by new members to join?

Maybe it has to do with an internal sense of the legitimacy of the group? After all, is this not what we say about the position of the psychoanalyst—that when all is said and done, it is an internal position one must find within oneself in order to become a psychoanalyst?

In short, the success of the group is about a "Desire" for psychoanalysis in Iran.

I was surprised to discover that this desire for psychoanalysis in Iran is not a new phenomenon; it has always been there. Many of Freud's writings were translated into Farsi as early as 1906; some of his books were translated into Farsi before they were translated into French. And yet nothing systematic has come out of it and it is as if this desire remains fragmented, not finding its way towards a cohesive becoming. It would be a fantastic study to find out why. When I look at the current situation, and this boom in psychoanalysis that we are observing in Iran, I also feel that every step of the way, this desire is turning into a defense against this very desire. For example, there is a tendency now in Iran toward the "universitization" of psychoanalysis, which I find very problematic.

I also find some of the fees that are being charged absurd: it is a commodification of psychoanalysis, based on a clear market logic of supply and demand: "I have something you really want, it's almost becoming a brand of its own; it's called psychoanalysis. There are still very few psychoanalysts in Iran, so if you want me, you will pay whatever fee I demand."

Once a colleague responded to my critique of such absurd fees by saying "But it is my desire to be rich, and one should follow one's desire, isn't this what well-analyzed subjects are supposed to be like?" I always thought that one could make a really good living out of this profession, but somehow I am afraid that if you want to become rich out of practicing psychoanalysis, you

DOI: 10.4324/9781003269113-10

are lurking in perverse territory. It seems to me that you might then be in the wrong profession. Psychoanalysts work with a sliding fee, meaning that a fee will be agreed between analyst and analysands depending on many different factors; and this logic is one that is based on the workings of the unconscious mind, and one that is loaded with material for the analytic process.

I find it disturbing when in Iran the norm is that the fee is told to the interested person who calls to get an appointment; and they are also told that if they can't afford the fee, they shouldn't even come in for a consultation. If one wants to work as a psychoanalyst, one has to believe in the unconscious. And, also, what a bizarre case load it would make! To filter out anyone who cannot afford high fees. *No* fee can compensate for a relatively homogeneous caseload. I am aware that every human being is unique, and so on, and that is certainly true. However, I believe that filtering out many groups in society because, for example, they cannot afford your very high fee will be a great intellectual loss for the analyst as well. So it is not in the name of charity that I am recommending sliding fees for analysts, but in the name of the unconscious.

I established the Freudian Group of Tehran in 2007, to function as a psychoanalytic institute, in which we attempt to practice the tripartite IPA regulations for the training of candidates: analysis, supervision, and theory classes. For the past several years, we have been the fortunate recipients of the hospitality of many of our international colleagues, and the observers of the most desiring eyes of our candidates over time.

Now, I will elaborate on various aspects of doing psychoanalysis in Tehran—not necessarily related on the manifest level, but with the intention of giving you a feel for doing psychoanalysis in Tehran.

To understand psychoanalysis in a specific geographical context: this is the role of the IPA group Geographies of Psychoanalysis, in which our attempt is as Lorena Preta, the founder and director of the group, expresses:

> We are not talking about adopting relativism, which instead of favoring contact isolates every thought and culture in its own particular dimension, but making anthropological models dynamic, including those in the Western world where psychoanalysis was born, and then putting them in contact with others with their respective problem areas of the present day. In this sense, psychoanalysis must not be transplanted but "put to work" in the various contexts, in its dual role towards psychoanalysis and also outwards, in such a way that it may also highlight any changes that cultural influence causes both to the models and to the clinical aspects.[1]

We have also experienced an increasing "mixing-up" of various analytic relationships. (Many are in class and in faculty meetings with their analyst, many people in the group know each other and have relationships with each other outside of the group, such as in the workplace.) This creates an even more challenging atmosphere than usual to combat our own and our candidates' seductive defenses against unconscious fantasy. It makes it easier to drown in reality, and reality alone. A very imposing, harsh, and persecutory socio-political reality, for that matter.

In order to escape to some extent from challenges such as incestuous relationships within our group, we have attempted to open up the group to the outside world. We have encouraged our students/candidates to improve their language skills, to get supervision and analysis from abroad. As such, we have welcomed many visiting colleagues every year, and classes are offered via international analysts on Skype.

Yet we often find students/candidates to be jacks-of-all-trades, but masters of none. Perhaps this is a symptom of contemporary psychoanalysis in general, but it becomes a serious problematic within the new territory that is psychoanalysis in Iran. Could this, again, be a question of the general psychoanalytic education of our times? I tend to think that could be true, and yet it seems thornier in the situation of psychoanalysis in Iran.

It does not seem that for the time being this has led toward an integration of various theories, although it has on some occasions. Mostly it has led to an imitation of various parts of different theories, not what one would call an internalization. In such cases I do not see the liberation, integration, and creativity that could come from such a way of being.

There are added cultural elements that I find helpful to keep in mind as we attempt to put our psychoanalytic discourse to work within a specific geography.

Just to give you an example: I find that the interesting idea of psychoanalytic reverie can in Iran easily become confused and mixed up with a sense of intuition in a country where there is a fascinating ancient and ingrained cultural tradition of mysticism and Sufism. There exists a familiarity towards being a shaman rather than being a psychoanalyst: this is certainly a familiar resistance toward the unconscious, but it becomes very context-specific and not such a long way from the discourse read in the tea leaves: "You have a voyage ahead of you: you will have three kids, and a long life." But, paradoxically, I must also say that there is an enigmatic desire for psychoanalysis in Iran which I have not observed in many other places.

Along these lines, it seems that in countries such as Iran, it is almost impossible to escape a socio-political psychoanalytic discourse and to hide behind our couches, which can be more easily done in some other countries. I would say perhaps this makes Iran similar to the United States since 2016, and especially under the Trump administration. This hiding is the reason why, even though much has been written about the politics of psychoanalysis and about the psychoanalysis of politics, there is little to be found in the literature about the socio-political context of the analytic practice, and about the impact of political events outside of the analytic situation onto the analytic process inside the session.

My question is: How would a major political crisis in wider society affect the unfolding of the analytic process within the session?

For example, after the presidential elections in Iran on 12 June 2009, when the announced result of the election was not accepted by many Iranians, a people's movement, the Green Movement, was formed, which for a short time brought a great deal of political uproar to the streets of Iran. This political uproar outside affected my patients differently. Some were oblivious to the events outside of the analytic situation, while others experienced a great deal of internal turmoil that disturbed the ambiance of their sessions.

Clearly one reacts to any socio-political event according to one's own intra/ interpsychic structures. Yet as my clinical observations in the session suggest, traumatic political events outside the room tend to provoke feelings of help-lessness, fears of being attacked, annihilated, and also a regression in the subject inside the analytic room.

A regression into a symbiotic state, and a need to enter into a narcissistic transference, elaborated mostly in terms of taking sides, splitting, and an increasing feeling of "us against them." The questions which stand out across all my data of that time are: "How alike are we? How hard is it to tolerate being with someone who is not like me? How do I understand the idea of me/ not me?" And, finally: "Are you on my side or their side?"

In a sense, the communication to the analyst seems to be: in order for you to understand me, you need to be on my side, and in order for me to feel you are on my side, you need to be exactly like me, and so you can understand me only if you are a replica of me.

To go through the clinical data I have received from the six different clin-icians would be beyond the scope of this book.

Volkan's work, one of the most detailed psychoanalytic descriptions of the *we-ness* schema, points to a human need to have enemies as well as allies, a need connected to the developmental processes of childhood. Volkan stresses the importance of the stranger anxiety in the development of the "enemy" concept. In his view, danger is experienced through the child's hostile destructiveness and rage toward his or her mother. Because the child cannot afford to lose the mother's love, rage is displaced onto an external object—the stranger—even though the stranger has never attacked the baby. Following Spitz, Volkan argues: "The actual identity of the stranger does not matter; what does matter is who the stranger is not."[2] This results in a precursor of the individualized idea of enemy.

In times of violent conflict, when there is a concrete threat to the existence of life, there is a regression to a primitive mode of thinking. When this hap-pens, the subject's obsession becomes primarily a desire to defend oneself against the other, and to relate to one's own group.

In a sense, the communication to the analyst elaborated in the data I received seems to function in the service of a need for recognition, understanding, and support: you need to be on my side, and in order for me to feel you are on my side, you need to be exactly like me. In fact, you can understand me only if you are me!

In today's world it has become increasingly challenging to hide behind our analytic couches and to practice armchair psychoanalysis in my geography and in yours. Psychoanalysts must stay faithful to the Freudian discourse of never taking sides while betraying their (sometimes visible) agoraphobic symptoms, and must occasionally leave their consulting rooms.

As soon as I say this, I am also aware of how all that is going on outside our analytic offices has also become a resistance to the unconscious in recent years; for example, I also sometimes wonder: are psychoanalysts working at all inside their offices? Or: the more turbulent the geopolitics of the outside world becomes, the more we are drawn to the reality of that outside world, destabilizing our psychoanalytic minds.

Certainly, we have to keep in mind that one cannot make such sharp distinctions between inside and outside; that they are correlated and on a continuum.

Yet the most magnificent thing about *doing psychoanalysis in Tehran* is that it allows me to practice it in its original, subversive, revolutionary form.

Living in Iran and working there as a psychoanalyst allows one to see and hear things through one's third eye and ear, and to find meanings through these broken/accented lines.

The language of the unconscious is the language of the margin: it is subversive, and it must remain so. The moment psychoanalysis becomes solely a mainstream discourse, a discourse of the center, we are normalizing it, we are assimilating it, and it is no longer the discourse of the unconscious. We need to be reminded of what Freud said: that if one day we speak about psychoanalysis and do not get angry or hostile reactions to it, that is a clear sign that we have not done a good job of explaining what psychoanalysis really is.[3] It is a clear sign that we have become mainstream: moved away from the margins, from unconscious fantasy and into the unfearful territory of sameness and familiarity. Maybe the crisis of psychoanalysis in the West has to do with this very phenomenon; maybe the harder we tried to fit psychoanalysis into the capitalist motto "the customer is always right," maybe the more we tried to cleanse it of anything that made anyone feel uncomfortable, such as unconscious fantasy, sexuality, and... in short, maybe the more politically correct we became in order to attract "customers," the less desirable we became for analysands. We became mainstream to make ourselves more attractive but, alas, we lost all desirability and mystery in the process, did we not? In Iran, psychoanalysis is still an uncannily Caliban profession, and I certainly hope to be able to keep it as such.

Notes

1 Flipping Book, "Overview Geographies_2019."
2 Volkan, "The Need to Have Enemies and Allies."
3 Freud, "Analysis Terminable and Interminable."

In Praise of the Reality Principle, or, In Praise of Disturbance

At first sight there seems to be a clear antagonism between the Freudian pleasure principle and the reality principle. The former is associated—I believe incorrectly—with the pleasure-seeking goal, while the reality principle is almost moral, with all kinds of impositions into the abstention from pleasure. But there is a fundamental metapsychological misunderstanding in such conclusions, which in my opinion has had disastrous consequences for psychoanalysis.

Freud clearly argued that both the reality principle and the pleasure principle are in search of pleasure.

> An ego thus educated has become "reasonable"; it no longer lets itself be governed by the pleasure principle, but obeys the reality principle, which also, at bottom, seeks to obtain pleasure, but pleasure which is assured through taking account of reality, even though it is pleasure postponed and diminished.[1]

But reasonableness and ego have had the worst reputations in psychoanalysis.

Granted, this might be a caricature of how we develop a mind, but we cannot forget that caricatures are powerful tools, so here it goes:

We start from a pure culture of the pleasure principle, of primary process, in the land of sensations, where we are one with our mothers, when she feeds us the moment that we are hungry; she is supposed to intuitively pick this up. We don't even have to communicate our needs. Our maternal object is there at our beck-and-call, we are one and the same with her, sharing a body; she has no desires of her own, no desire outside of us. "I want it and I want it now" is the id's declaration at this stage, according to Freud.[2]

Then—hopefully, but not too early—there comes a moment when the infant's hunger is not responded to immediately; she is shocked, disturbed, and she cries and cries, and this leads to her hallucinating the breast, and the milk, but to no avail. Alas, this hallucination, though comforting for a little while, does not fill her stomach. This very notion is the inauguration of the reality principle, of its initiation to the psyche, when the infant realizes that

DOI: 10.4324/9781003269113-11

hallucinating the breast/bottle does not make her hunger go away. How does this disturbing stage become possible? Through frustration, through the absence of the maternal object. If the maternal object is present at all times, and never frustrates the infant, how does the infant ever get to move to the hallucinatory phase, and then to the reality principle, where concepts of time and space are introduced for the first time, where she begins to develop a mind? How can the maternal object perform this function of disturbance? Via a third, and only a third, which simply means having other desires outside the child.

Soon the infant begins to fantasize: "Ah, she is not feeding me the moment that I feel hungry, I must learn to communicate my needs to her. It is not simply that I feel it and she magically knows it." This is the very early seed of separation, and the seed also of a narcissistic injury to our primary narcissism. This is where we say farewell to the danger of melancholia(s) to come after, this is where the seed of finding a lighthouse and then of becoming a lighthouse of our own becomes a possibility, in the midst of the dark, turbulent seas that await us all. A built-in lighthouse, so to speak, that will help our Odysseus to navigate through dark and stormy seas.

As time goes by, more intense and excruciating narcissistic injuries will, with any luck, come our way. The baby wonders about the absence of the mother: where is she? And, more importantly, with whom? Here we are thrown into the inauguration of Oedipus, of a proper triangulation, leading to bewilderment: what was missing in me that led to such a betrayal on the maternal object's part? This possibility to acknowledge a lack, this excruciatingly painful realization, is our only vehicle to thinking, creativity, language and most definitely to pleasure.

It is indeed pleasure that is delayed and diminished. But this is the only possible definition of pleasure; a pleasure that is not delayed, that is not diminished, is beyond the pleasure principle, within the territory of *jouissance à la* Lacan and crossing into the death drive; unbound, according to Freud. So our only possible access to pleasure is via the reality principle, via having been disturbed, having been frustrated and having faced absence.

Certainly there is a level of frustration that can become lethal for the undifferentiated little infant, but over my years of practicing psychoanalysis I have come to the conclusion that more people are suffering from mothers who never left, who were too involved, who had no desire outside their children, even to the point where they did not even desire their partners, than vice versa. This does not mean that it should not be acknowledged that, early on, the infant needs to feel undifferentiated and fused with the maternal object in order to develop a secure attachment: the phase that Winnicott calls "primary maternal preoccupation" is necessary as a building block to the possibility of a healthy separation later on.[3] It is merely that he says there are mothers who for various reasons are incapable of achieving this state, meaning that they lack the tolerance for a brief psychotic episode, while using the "flight to sanity" as a defense. That is indeed true; however I consider that we also have to acknowledge and highlight the mothers who never find their way back to sanity and insist on a never-ending, non-separated phase with their children eternally. In such cases, I recommend the defense of a "flight to sanity" as something that could be useful indeed.

It seems to me that sometimes our patients and perhaps some contemporary psychoanalysts deem that the primary maternal preoccupation phase needs to last until death do us part.

These concepts, however, are not so markedly unrelated. It seems that those primary maternal objects that never leave are indeed the ones that, paradoxically, were never truly present to begin with: they remained fused with their infant as a defense against being truly present for that infant. It is clear that you can work your way to absence only if you have been present for the required amount of time, both in quality and in quantity. If you are not connected to your infant, you will never be able to be absent, and will remain in a fusion of your own, in an absent presence, in a non-subjective undifferentiation, without ever finding the pleasure of meeting/greeting the beings we and our children actually are, missing out on this most exciting encounter.

It cannot escape us that it is via the reality principle that we are saved from hallucinatory psychosis as a structure, for dreaming, and art, are possible only through landing on the shoulders of the reality principle. As we know, psychotics don't dream, and the magic of Alice in Wonderland becomes possible only because she knows, every step of the way, that there is a way out of the rabbit hole. If one momentarily imagines Alice to be forever stuck in Wonderland, if one imagines an Alice who never wakes up, well, then all the magic is certainly gone, all the pleasure, and we are back to re-finding our very own melancholia.

So the picture of melancholia is the picture of a regression to primary narcissism, of denying reality, of the concreteness of psychosis, where we still believe in magical thinking and have not reached magic. We know that rebellion against the constraints of the reality principle, in favor of a belief in infantile omnipotence, appears as a feature of all neurotic behavior. Freud argued, however, that "there is a path that leads back from phantasy to reality—the path, that is, of art."[4] Perhaps the secret is in the possibility of this back-and-forth. Leading back is the key word: *back*; there has been a voyage to reality, and now we will have the luxury of temporarily abandoning it, as we do in dreams, and in extraordinary art. Abandoning it to pink elephants, unicorns, flying cows, and watch-holding, tea-drinking rabbits. To animals that speak, kisses that transform a frog into a prince. To magic carpets and lamps, and houses made of chocolate. Pleasures which are the possible merit of the back-and-forth within the domain of the reality principle.

In the pages to come I will repetitively emphasize my claim on the value of disturbances, of the reality principle, and of absence. For within the Freudian metapsychology it is absolutely impossible to develop a mind without the absence of the other. This is strikingly elaborated in the game that Freud's little grandson plays, *Fort/Da*. (I touched upon this in the earlier chapter on Caliban.)

In his paper on "Negation," Freud posits two kinds of judgments: the judgment of existence and the judgment of attribution; the latter comes down to a question of whether a thing has a particular attribute or not.[5] To follow Freud's text: judgment is an intellectual activity that "affirms or disaffirms the possession by a thing of a particular attribute; and it asserts or disputes that a presentation has an existence in reality." It is a question, then, of giving something that is at first perceived to be the judgment of existence, with each successive perception thereby entailing a re-finding of the original perception. Freud goes on to say:

> The antithesis between subjective and objective does not exist from the first. It only comes into being from the fact that thinking possesses the capacity to bring before the mind once more something that has once been perceived, by reproducing it as a presentation without the external object having still to be there. The first and immediate aim, therefore, of reality-testing is not to find an object in real perception which corresponds to the one presented, but to re-find such an object, to convince oneself that it is still there.

Such postulations will certainly lead to fundamental differences in child-rearing approaches. For example, I would value the power of delayed gratification, of impulse control, of independence, of containing the child's anxiety by providing limits and containments. We are all afraid of our own wishes, which might lead to a great deal of anxiety and a hallucinatory belief in the omnipotent powers we think we possess. What if, in the name of love, you are not provided with limits? What if you can have that sixth ice-cream, if you can buy whatever you want, if you don't have to do anything you don't want to do? What if you never have to be separated from your maternal object because she is always there, always present, never allowing you to discover the pleasures of hide-and-seek, for she is never hiding, always in clear view? This will lead to a complete and extremely dangerous enslavement of passionless mothers and psychically dead children. It is terrifying to think that the contemporary discourse around maternity promotes this exact chilling scenario between mothers and their children, and that historically it has always done so.

Moreover, such assumptions lead to drastic differences within the psychoanalytic clinic, from analysts who try to be as present as possible, who time many of their interpretations around the break, the weekend, the vacations, the missing session; who constantly worry about their patient's level of frustration; who do not want to even make an interpretation, for after all any interpretation is disturbing; who incessantly employ a parallel vocabulary to the parent/child dynamic within the transference/countertransference dynamics; to those who are too compromising when it comes to limits and, ultimately, when it comes to being there to repair a fragile and broken patient, certainly via the analyst's all-powerful gifts.

It goes without saying that this is not a promotion of a sadomasochistic dynamic, or of deliberate frustrations and no regard for the level of the anxiety of the patient, and, as I mentioned above, I am aware of the caricatural nature of my claims.

Right across contemporary psychoanalytic clinical cases, we hear theories of curing through love and "presence," and certainly no one could disagree with that. Our more primitive patients are particularly in need of it, and I believe this is why there is a clear bias in some analytic schools toward interpretations which address the breaks in treatment, the times between the sessions, vacations, and weekends, all with very good results. However, I find—and perhaps this is a more general critique of mine toward contemporary psychoanalysis—that we forget the absolutely essential value of "absence" for developing a mind. And that separation anxiety is often about closeness to the object and the fear of being engulfed by it, of wanting to leave the object but being terrified of how vengeful she might become if we realize our wish to separate.

We need to be fundamentally disturbed in order to develop the capacity to hallucinate a breast/bottle, and thus to get closer to the reality principle through which we can exit our primary narcissism and enter what André Green has exquisitely named the "objectilizing function of the drive."[6] For Green,

> the essential function of the life drive is to ensure an objectilizing function. This does not simply mean that its role is to form a relation with the object (internal and external) but that it is capable of transforming structures into an object, even when the object is no longer directly involved.

I find that analysts are often too present, talking too much, afraid of dropping a helpless infant, and ultimately trying to heal her through presence, not thought. I do not hold the view that we can heal our own wounds or those of our patients, but I think we can find the courage to name our wounds, to live a pleasurable life not despite our wounds, but because of them. We can enter this shaky, scary territory of love, with no guarantees, only if we become interested in leaving our infantile, fusional paradises in favor of binding our libido to the outside world, outside of our selves. The method and clinical stance that analysts often take these days is a method of feeding. I think there is a difference between feeding the patient and overfeeding her because we are afraid she is going to die. Probably something in the middle of these two theoretical standings would be best, but such ideal treatment also belongs to our lost paradises, so I should not be seduced into expecting such a paradise the very moment I am advising against the possibility of such havens. In the final analysis, I am promoting not a devaluing of the maternal preoccupations of the analytic position, but the importance of also keeping in mind the value of the paternal function. I found it delightful to read about an extensive recent study which showed that more insecure attachments in therapists led to a more empathic style of therapies.

And, by the way, the reality principle is not moral but merely ethical, for we know very well that the superego is closest to the id. For the more we follow our id's unlimited, unrestrained, unbound ecstasy-seeking wishes, the more we become slaves to the imprisoning, deadening sado-masochism of our superegos.

Lewis Kirshner writes, as he elaborates towards an ethics in psychoanalysis:

> Man is a wolf to his fellow man, Freud famously quoted Plautus in *Civilization and Its Discontents*, and his neighborly intentions are an amalgam of conflicting motives and fears. The analyst's therapeutic zeal is no exception to this caution, risking as it does the imposition of his own fantasies and beliefs on a vulnerable patient. The ethical form of this Freudian message is reprised by Jonathon Lear. When trying to intervene to correct a problem, how does the analyst avoid applying his own personal reality and personal desire to his patient? So Lacan's emphasis, while going somewhat further in this direction, was not unique in its insistence that the mere attempt to do good, to help, can lead analysts astray:
>
> > At every moment we need to know what our effective relationship is to the desire to do good, to the desire to cure. We have to deal with that as if it were something that is likely to lead us astray, and in many cases to do so instantly. I will even add that one might be paradoxical or trenchant and designate our desire as a non-desire to cure.[7]

I believe all of this to be in praise of the reality principle, part of the unconscious institution of the ego and hence the strength of the ego: but why does the ego have a bad reputation? If only it had a French name... if only it was not associated with American psychoanalysis; or, even better, if only it had an exotic Persian name; should we call it *"Nafs"*? What if we persisted, with a non-dogmatic faithfulness, in preserving our basic psychoanalytic premises that to some might seem old-school? It seems nowadays there is nothing more avant-garde, more contemporary, more subversive, in psychoanalysis than an insistence on some metapsychological foundation of Freudian psychoanalysis.

I trust one arrives at a non-authoritarian, original, passionate, and free state of mind if one's heritage is acknowledged and, I would even go as far as to say, loved.

Personally, I am an unfashionable Freudian analyst. This does not mean that one idealizes Freud, but it does mean that one works with the basic

Freudian metapsychological premises, and stays faithful to the subversive nature of psychoanalysis, which certainly holds a great deal more than the relationship between the two analytic subjects. Here, the body still matters not only as what it becomes, but also as something that is born. Here—just to name a few examples—there is a clear understanding of the significance of the drives, of unconscious fantasy; here, psychoanalysis is still about infantile sexuality, free association, and interpretations; here, perversion is the negative of neurosis, and neurosis comes out of the nucleolus of the Oedipus complex. Here, the work with psychotic patients is completely different, although there is certainly a psychotic, pre-Oedipal part in every single one of us. Here, dreams are central; psychoanalysis is not so much about self-disclosures as it is about self-restraints... here, we still work with castration: not as a degrading, politically incorrect concept toward women, but as the symbolic representation of the unavoidable lack within both sexes, albeit differently elaborated for each. Here, one believes that repetition compulsion, repression, and transference account for most of what the patient brings to the room.

Here, unconscious wishes are fears... And, most importantly, our analytic position is not about infantilizing our analysands to death, in a re-enactment of a wish to have no disturbance, no separation, no Oedipus complex, but only comfort, worry about the analysands' anxieties, and ultimately the wish to be nice human beings and to heal their injuries through love. This might represent the re-enactment of our wish to stay unseparated, undifferentiated, in an undisturbed paradise with our maternal objects.

This, for Kristeva, is the essence of melancholia: when we cannot mourn the loss of our maternal objects, when we cannot face the reality of matricide, we are bound to fall into the bottomless abyss of the dark sun of melancholia.[8]

Hence, can we go as far as to say that contemporary psychoanalysis has become melancholic? Well, it certainly has all the symptoms; where there is no sexuality, no fathers, only pre-Oedipal issues, the body is really not a body of one's own but one which we share with our maternal object. We have moved further and further away from thinking, where there is time and space, into a territory of pre-Oedipal, predominantly early, narcissistic issues, where we resist disturbance. This wish for paradise, for the sun, has led us straight into the blackness of melancholia, into a regression to primary narcissism, into a lack of interest in the outside world, an absence of the objectilizing function of the drive à la André Green, one of the last psychoanalytic giants of our times. Where we have indeed repressed Freud's assertion to his Protestant pastor friend: "It is necessary to become a bad individual, to transform, to renounce... Without a bit of evil character," he continued, "there is no true result."[9]

Hate and aggression seem to be a necessary part of many creative acts. Winnicott elaborates that creativity implies a capacity for ruthlessness, a disregard for the object, a lack of concern for it: "[It is the artist's ruthlessness that] does in fact... achieve more than guilt-driven labour."[10]

I am reminded of a marvelous little book by Alphonse Daudet: *La Doulou*, the Provencal word for the French *douleur*, pain. He was a true man of letters, and always had been. *In the Land of Pain* (the English translation of the title) is a collection of notes where Daudet chronicles the pain and suffering he experienced from *tabes dorsalis*.[11]

There is a passage in the book where he is sixteen and his brother Henri dies, at which moment their father gives vent to a great howl of "He is dead! He is dead!" Daudet was aware of his bifurcated response to this event:

> My first Me was in tears, but my second Me was thinking, what a terrific cry! It would be really good in the theatre! [...] I've often thought about this dreadful duality. This terrible second Me is always there, sitting in a chair watching, while the first Me stands up, performs actions, lives, suffers, struggles away. This second Me that I've never been able to get drunk, or make cry, or to put to sleep. And how much he sees into things! And how he mocks!

The worst analytic position for a melancholic is that of a humanitarian, a nice analyst who tries gently to convince his melancholic patient that he is not bad. This approach, as we know, could very well at times even lead our melancholic patients to commit suicide, and we should also be aware of curing melancholia too fast for the sudden liberation of all that cathected libido, which can abruptly turn melancholia into a very dangerous and out-of-control mania: yet another example of the eagerness of our good analysts to cure which could have dreadful consequences. All in all, it seems that it could be highly recommended to psychoanalytic clinicians to keep their "goodness" under scrutiny at all times.

Here again we should follow Freud when, in "Mourning and Melancholia," he says:

> It would be equally fruitless from a scientific and a therapeutic point of view to contradict a patient who brings these accusations against his ego [...] He also seems to us justified in certain other self-accusations; it is merely that he has a keener eye for the truth than other people who are not melancholic. When in his heightened self-criticism he describes himself as petty, egoistic, dishonest, lacking in independence, one whose sole aim has been to hide the weaknesses of his own nature, it may be, so far as we know, that he has come pretty near to understanding himself; we only wonder why a man has to be ill before he can be accessible to a truth of this kind. For there can be no doubt that if anyone holds and expresses to others an opinion of himself such as this (an opinion which Hamlet held both of himself and of everyone else: "Use every man after his desert, and who shall scape whipping?" (Act II, Scene 2)), he is ill, whether he is speaking the truth or whether he is being more or less unfair to himself.[12]

It is in the above 1917 paper, "Mourning and Melancholia," one of Freud's most Shakespearian works, that he attempts to elaborate on pathological melancholia as opposed to mourning. Basically he searches to find an elaboration of the Blues: "Mourning is regularly the reaction to the loss of a loved person, or to the loss of some abstraction which has taken the place of one, such as one's country, liberty, an ideal, and so on." The same factors, Freud tells us, produce melancholia in some people.

He goes on to say that in both cases, mourning and melancholia, there is a cessation of interest in the outside world, inhibitions on all activity, and a loss of the capacity to love. There is, however, one fascinating exception in melancholia: we observe a significant lowering of self-regard. This dialectic of crime and punishment is absent in mourning. Freud goes on to enlighten us on the economics of pain:

> Profound mourning, the reaction to the loss of someone who is loved, contains the same painful frame of mind, the same loss of interest in the outside world—in so far as it does not recall him—the same loss of capacity to adopt any new object of love (which would mean replacing him) and the same turning away from any activity that is not connected with thoughts of him. It is easy to see that this inhibition and circumscription of the ego is the expression of an exclusive devotion to mourning which leaves nothing over for other purposes or other interests. It is really only because we know so well how to explain it that this attitude does not seem to us pathological.

Other fundamental differences are touchingly elaborated by Freud in "Mourning and Melancholia," such as that the melancholic only knows whom he has lost but not *what* he has lost: "This would suggest that melancholia is in some way related to an object-loss which is withdrawn from consciousness, in contradistinction to mourning, in which there is nothing about the loss that is unconscious."

> In mourning it is the world which has become poor and empty; in melancholia it is the ego itself.
> [...]
> This picture of a delusion of (mainly moral) inferiority is completed by sleeplessness and refusal to take nourishment, and—what is psychologically very remarkable—by an overcoming of the instinct which compels every living thing to cling to life.

But the melancholic is not ashamed to expose such a worthless self in front of other people; on the contrary, he seems to gain pleasure from the exhibition and self-exposure of it.

The essential thing, therefore, is not whether the melancholic's distressing self-denigration is correct, in the sense that his self-criticism agrees with the opinion of other people. The point must rather be that he is giving a correct description of his psychological situation. He has lost his self-respect and he must have good reason for this. It is true that we are then faced with a contradiction that presents a problem which is hard to solve. The analogy with mourning led us to conclude that he had suffered a loss in regard to an object; what he tells us points to a loss in regard to his ego.

So the melancholic's ego has split, and one part has revolted against the other. We see how one part of the ego sets itself against the other, judges it critically, and, as it were, takes it as its object. This critical agency within the ego becomes what Freud later called the superego. But upon a closer look at each clinical picture, we perceive that these self-reproaches are reproaches against a loved object, which have been shifted away from it on to the patient's own ego.

Their complaints are really "plaints" in the old sense of the word. They are not ashamed and do not hide themselves, since everything derogatory that they say about themselves is at bottom said about someone else. Moreover, they are far from evincing towards those around them the attitude of humility and submissiveness that would alone befit such worthless people. On the contrary, they make the greatest nuisance of themselves, and always seem as though they felt slighted and had been treated with great injustice.

Freud goes on to explain:

Thus the shadow of the object fell upon the ego, and the latter could henceforth be judged by a special agency, as though it were an object, the forsaken object. In this way an object-loss was transformed into an ego-loss and the conflict between the ego and the loved person into a cleavage between the critical activity of the ego and the ego as altered by identification. [...] It represents, of course, a regression from one type of object-choice to original narcissism. We have elsewhere shown that identification is a preliminary stage of object-choice, that it is the first way—and one that is expressed in an ambivalent fashion—in which the ego picks out an object. The ego wants to incorporate this object into itself, and, in accordance with the oral or cannibalistic phase of libidinal development in which it is, it wants to do so by devouring it.

Let us finish our "Praise of Disturbance" with two recent dreams recounted by Mr. E, the aforementioned patient from Azerbaijan, which, somehow, humorously encapsulate his howls of the Blues to come.

The first dream

> We were supposed to have a scientific meeting, like a congress. I walk in and the topic is the death of the father, so I leave right away *screaming* "This is not my meeting, I don't belong here!" and I sort of run away outside towards Professor K. He has a deep wound in his foot which I try to make better by washing it away with water, but every time I wash it, the wound comes back, now that I am thinking of it, sort of like how the water of the sea would wash away my sandcastles, leaving me to face a wound over and over again. In the dream, Professor K looks at me and he says: "It's very painful, but let's go get an *ice-cream*."

And the second dream

> I got into a plane twice. Both times, the plane fell for various technical reasons, yet nothing happened to me or any of the other passengers, but I knew I would somehow get on that third plane; this made me anxious. I thought, something will definitely happen this third time around, will I survive the third plane? I was not sure, right before getting on the third plane, the anxiety got so intense that I woke up.

Leaving aside the many associations of the patient, the countless, complicated, and multifaceted layers of interpretations possible, and the many months we spent working on these very two dreams, as I listened to E's dreams and his associations in that session on that day in August, I thought that he needed to board that third plane, via a third, for this is the only possible transit route to transform our screams to *I-scream* to becoming an "I," towards the land of pleasures of the various shades of blues to come. This, quite contrary to the at-times popular assumption, does not mean that we have to give up the childish pleasures indicated in E's *ice-cream* metaphor. Getting on that third plane undoubtedly has turbulences of its own, but not getting on that plane, because our dream work fails us, will only allow us to crash in a small village named Melancholia, with absolutely no possibility of flying again, for this small village does not have an airport.

Notes

1 Freud, *Introductory Lectures on Psychoanalysis*.
2 Freud, *The Ego and the Id*.
3 Winnicott, *The Collected Works of D.W. Winnicott: Volume 5*.
4 Freud, *Introductory Lectures on Psychoanalysis*.
5 Freud, "Negation," 235–239.
6 Green, *The Work of the Negative*.
7 Kirshner, "Toward an Ethics of Psychoanalysis: A Critical Reading of Lacan's Ethics."
8 Kristeva, *Black Sun*.

9 Brown, "A Look at Oskar Pfister and His Relationship to Sigmund Freud."
10 Winnicott, cited in Kohon, *No Lost Certainties to Be Recovered: Sexuality, Creativity, Knowledge.*
11 Daudet, *In the Land of Pain.*
12 Freud, "Mourning and Melancholia," 237–258.

Against Empath"ism"[1]

Whatever the relationship between human mimicry and animal mimicry, and regardless of how mimicry is defined (the action or skill of imitating in order to entertain or ridicule, close external resemblances, what evolves around hiding and camouflage) or how it is referred to ("a world of impostures"), each and every time one is in danger of falling into the trap of pretending to be something one authentically is not, hence the signifier of mimicry is always somehow within the realm of the "superficial." Superficiality seems to be the most recognizable representative, where resemblance owing to mimicry is concerned!

Let us distinguish between this pretentious, superficial banality, and the superficiality which Nietzsche celebrated and praised: "what [...] is at the surface, the fold, the skin [...] the appearance, the forms and the words!"[2] The superficiality which goes hand-in-hand with mimicry is the one that ignores the complexity, depth, and darkness of humankind.

How are we to relate mimicry and empathy?

Mimicry is diverse, multifaceted, and complex, and so is empathy. If we use the animal world's predatory mimicry and defensive mimicry as metaphors, we become aware that sometimes mimicry is used in order to hide from the predator, and sometimes in order to take the prey by surprise and to overcome it.

The distinction between aggressive mimicry and predator camouflage depends on the signal given to the prey, which is not easily determined. Aggressive mimicry is opposite in principle to defensive mimicry, where the mimic generally benefits from being treated as harmful. In short, aggressive mimicry is predatory.

Both mechanisms can be seen in human relations, and different kinds of empathies can be observed accordingly. Empathy can be manipulative and close to predatory mimicry: I have an understanding of who my object is, and I will use it to "eat" my prey in order to feed myself. Examples of spies trying to understand "The Lives of Others" in the 2006 German film of that title, and undercover cops acting like gangsters in order to catch their prey in the act, are quite relevant to this kind of mimicry.[3] But this pretending could go

DOI: 10.4324/9781003269113-12

so deep that empathy might prevent them from accomplishing their original mission. This is a very interesting moment, an in-between moment: inside and outside, internal and external, between me / not me.

However, there is the other kind of mimicry which is usually intertwined with the negative kind of empathy; the one I like to call the "Parrot" kind! The message communicated in this case is: I have so much empathy for you that I want us to be exactly the same, a lookalike (see, for example, the film *Single White Female*, 1992).[4] It goes so far as to indicate that we are one shared body: no boundaries between us, no difference; we are skin to skin. This kind of fusion can end up forming a narcissistic "unit" that feels threatened by any kind of independence of one of the co/dependents, which might lead to the infamous "narcissistic injury" that cannot be tolerated by the "unit" manager in any shape or form! Defy me and I will destroy you, be like me, think like me, don't contradict me and I promise you the "world"; but, as one can imagine, this specific world is an Orwellian one…

As the prominent Italian psychoanalyst Stefano Bolognini informs us:

> True empathy is a condition of conscious and preconscious contact characterized by separateness, complexity, and a linked structure, a wide perceptual spectrum including every color in the emotional palette, from the lightest to the darkest; above all, it constitutes a progressive shared and deep contact with the complementarity of the object, with the other's defensive ego and split off parts no less than with his ego-syntonic subjectivity.[5]

The key word for genuine empathy lies within "separateness," within the essential capacity to recognize difference. Otherwise I am just getting to know you in order to prey upon you, so that I can eat you, for my insatiable narcissism needs to be fed over and over again.

This is where the determinant difference between speech and language comes into play; in this "Parrot" world, one can mime the words, or even mimic speech, but one cannot make an effective use of language as an instrument of communication between two subjects. This happens, for example, when people repeat a famous quote or concept, but remain without a voice when the first question is uttered by someone, such as: Why? How? What does that mean?

Often, they either babble and get into long, confusing, nonsensical sentences, or become voiceless…

The "Parrot" type of relationship does not allow for separation, and hence the possibility of subjectivity will remain a distant dream. This kind of mimicry is similar to the psychotic territory where Heideggerian "chatter" and Lacanian "empty speech" rules: a terrain that does not allow language to take form, since language comes via separation from the other, and via loss.

Mimicry is a developmental stage; and as such, no child should be fixated within its realm and each must move from it toward identification, and then dis-identification.

The child might very well wish to identify with parts of the mother or the father, but she should know that she is not her mother or her father, and that identifying with parts of them is a way of acknowledging their separateness, while mimicry can often mean becoming like others. Identification is the acceptance of loss and the awareness of separation. Mimicry, or introjection/ incorporation, is the defense against loss and its refusal.

Certainly, all of these things are nuanced, and should be looked at within a spectrum as staying faithful to the psychoanalytic premise "We are all everything." In short, often within mimicry there is no possibility of love or real empathy; in the land of the narcissist, even love or empathy is being mimicked; and the major question for the narcissist remains: What can your presence do for me? How can you feed my narcissism?

It is only in the realm of "separateness" that experiencing genuine empathy becomes a possibility. That is where and when time and space become identifiable concepts; only in identification/dis-identification and never in mimicry; and that is what leads to preservation and binding, not to un-binding and destruction…

Let us finish with a highly meaningful quote attributed to Jean-Luc Godard that beautifully encompasses the problematics of mimicry–empathy: "It's not where you take it from; it's where you take it to."[6]

Notes

1 This chapter is adapted with permission from a chapter in *Mimicry–Empathy*: Gohar Homayounpour (2020) "Against Empath'ism'," in *Mimicry–Empathy*, pp. 200–203, Berlin: Monroe Books.
2 Castle, *The Blackwell Guide to Literary Theory*.
3 Henckel von Donnersmarck, *Das Leben Der Anderen*.
4 Barbet Schroeder, *Single White Female*.
5 Atkins, "A Review of 'Psychoanalytic Empathy'."
6 Jarmusch, "Things I've Learned: Jim Jarmusch."

Forough

The year is 1962. I can imagine her entering my office, gently lying on the couch, her big black eyes immediately betraying a sense of both fragility and strength, a feathery light-darkness, all at the same time. In this narcissistic fantasy of mine I wonder what it would have been like to have Forough as an analysand. My narcissism does not stop there; it goes as far as to wonder if the finale of her life would have been any different if her tale could become a tale from a Freudian analyst's couch.

Forough Farrokhzad, the legendary Iranian poet and filmmaker, feminist, iconoclast, the most charismatic, avant-garde, and controversial figure in contemporary Iranian literature. Today, half a century after her untimely death in 1967 at the age of thirty-two, she is still very much part of the collective Iranian unconscious, a transgenerational phenomenon of the Iranian unconscious.

Forough is not at all nervous about being in a psychoanalyst's office; she tells me she has just gotten back from Tabriz after finishing a documentary film about people affected by leprosy, entitled *The House is Black*. She goes on to tell me that during the twelve days of shooting in Tabriz, she became fully attached to the child of two lepers, a boy named Hossein: "I have adopted the boy and brought him to live with me at my mother's house." I, the analyst, am clichéd enough to feel surprised to discover that Forough, symbol of female independence, rebellion, and freedom, lives with her *mother*.

She tells me, with a joyful fear: "I am here to get some help with my Hossein, I want to help him adapt to his new life."

I feel guilty for my clichéd thought. I remember the delightful Indian psychoanalyst Sudhir Kakar telling me time after time that Western psychoanalysis has gotten the idea of subjectivity which is the goal of psychoanalysis all wrong: the goal of psychoanalysis is not for you to become a subject, but for you to become a loving subject. Subjectivity, for Kakar, finds its ways home via the route of loving, otherwise it gets lost.

Little did I know then that guilt would become the main protagonist of my discourse with Forough; little did I know on that sunny afternoon in Tehran that Forough believed herself to be a criminal. What was her crime? The

DOI: 10.4324/9781003269113-13

punishment was crystal clear; the oracles of her unconscious had spoken early on: she was condemned to lull her death drive exactly five years after our meeting that day in March, when she died in a car accident. She swerved her jeep off the main road in order not to hit a school bus. She died saving children of kindergarten age, this impossible choice that she must have situated herself in: "To die, or to live and kill all those young kids?" This choice, which is no choice, after all, lets my associations loose.

I think of Lacan's famous example of the difference between the pleasure principle and *jouissance*, one he borrowed from Kant's *Critique of Practical Reason*, where Kant discusses a scenario in which a man is offered the chance to have sex with the woman of his dreams, but there is a catch: after such an indulgence, he will be hanged.[3] According to our dear Immanuel, who believed that reason is the source of morality, the choice is a clear one for our subject: he will, reasonably enough, renounce such a momentary pleasure of lust, for a mere experience of intercourse is never worth one's life, even with a woman that you have fantasized or longed for all your life.[4] The man will base his decision on the future price of a choice to submit to his natural, animalistic, sensual nature; our Kantian subject has the ability to transcend that. Here, the no to "lust" of our Kantian subject is due to the workings of the pleasure principle. As the pleasure principle works via the reality principle to obtain a balance sheet of pleasure and pain, always attempting to have more pleasure and less pain, so it is not the reality principle that is in antagonism with the pleasure principle, it is *jouissance* that is always ultimately an enemy of the pleasure principle. *Jouissance* is "beyond the pleasure principle, for it breaks off negotiations with the reality principle, in that it bypasses the moderating influence of the ego on the drives."[5]

So the night of sex does not make sense within the economics of the pleasure principle, but as we know very well from Freud's theories in *Beyond the Pleasure Principle*, we often unconsciously choose to repeat painful experiences over and over again. This is the repetition compulsion of neurotics; this is the work in which Freud comes to the conclusion that if we keep making unreasonable choices, choices that do not make sense within the economics of the pleasure principle, then there must be another drive that is antagonistic to life, to the binding powers of Eros: that which he names the unbounded Thanatos.

So our Freudian subject, unlike our Kantian subject, is very well capable of choosing a night of sexual pleasure with the ultimate object of his dream in return for his life. Our Freudian/Lacanian speculations go further than that: the woman becomes the woman of our subject's dreams upon the introduction of the possibility of being hanged after a night of sexual satisfaction with her. It is the sacrifice of life, of entering the territory of death, that is always beyond the pleasure principle. *Jouissance* is always, without a doubt, the workings of Thanatos. So the man chooses the night of sex with the woman not despite his impending death, but because of it.

I am reminded of a patient in analysis saying to his analyst:

> By now I know you will never have sex with me, but what if there were an earthquake while I am on the couch and we both knew that we would die in a few hours, would you have sex with me then?

Jouissance is always in the shadow of the death drive; it is beyond the pleasure principle, where we have broken off with reality and the economics of pleasure/pain. Slavoj Žižek explains:

> Lacan's counter-argument here is that we certainly do have to guess what his answer may be: what if we encounter a subject (as we do regularly in psychoanalysis) who can only enjoy a night of passion fully if some form of "gallows" is threatening him—that is, if, by doing it, he is violating some prohibition? ... if gratifying sexual passion involves the suspension of even the most elementary "egoistic" interests... this gratification is clearly located "beyond the pleasure principle."[6]

Let us, for just a moment, imagine the man who knows he has given up his life for the supposedly ultimate lady of his dreams: well, *jouissance* obtained is clearly, according to Lacan, different from *jouissance* expected. The woman of the man's dreams, in an actual sexual encounter, becomes covered in sweat, a real flesh-and-blood being. This is exactly the same as the absolute horror for a patient who actually gets to have sex with his/her analyst. We wish to obtain our incestuous desirable objects, but the moment we actually do, not in fantasy but in reality, we have crossed into the inferno "beyond the pleasure principle," crossing the border into the death drive.

Can we imagine a third choice (I always like third choices): can we imagine our Kantian/Freudian fallen hero walking away from this bizarre proposal in order to get a great cup of coffee, or go for a swim, to take his kid for a walk, to meet with dear friends for a delicious meal and great conversation? Again, I am entering unfashionable territory.

Can we imagine our guy, looking forward to going home to a *good-enough* sexual relationship with his wife, not nearly as often as he would like but often enough, or can we imagine him walking away to go to his girlfriend, a very ordinary woman of earthly qualities whom he has come to love over the years? He does not want to make her wait, for he knows how anxious she gets when he is late; he knows exactly what she will do, how her fantasies will run wild; he knows her fragile history, and for him no night of sexual passion with the woman of his dreams will be worth the pain of causing her anxiety, because he loves her.

He knows how the corners of her lips will twitch nervously, and how her forehead will bulge; how she will start to speak a bit more loudly than usual and move her hands ungracefully, obsessively calling his number over and over again.

Here again, within the Freudian realm, the point of these third choices for our imagined subject does not come from altruism, or from being a good, self-sacrificing human being, and it certainly does not come solely from a typical Kantian reasonableness. It comes from the pleasure principle. The man in our example is aware of the phantasmatic qualities of ultimate objects of desire, of the mirage that awaits him in that one night of promised perfect lust. And with Adam Phillips, and in the name of the pleasure principle, he has come to enjoy "unforbidden" pleasures, no longer bewitched by the shadow of the death drive that always inevitably accompanies forbidden pleasure.

For Phillips, we are being instructed what to desire by the forbidders, and that is truly a shame because most of our pleasures, like the pleasures of our childhood, are unforbidden. Is it not that the celebration of unforbidden pleasures is our visa out of the territory of the puritanism of guilt and the superego?[7] The moment the forbidders instruct us not to do something, a wish is created to do that exact forbidden deed—a tantalizing wish, according to Phillips. Hence, in our search for forbidden pleasures we are confirming that we are the slaves of the forbidders. He essentially says that rules and the temptation to break them confuse our sense of pleasure with notions of self-control. So, basically, when we are in the claws of taboos and forbidden pleasures, we are being obedient to the forbidders.

Thus, when it comes to forbidden pleasures, we are in the terrain of crime and punishment, in the plot of guilt for our forbidden wishes, and ultimately in the land of the sadomasochist, where pleasures always have the aroma of pain, and pleasure is eroticized death, sexualized pain.

I hope I am making it clear that this is not a moral stance, it is a stance on the side of the kaleidoscopic possibilities of the pleasure principle.

We do not want to know what we know, what we want, and the more troubling our desire, the more repressed it is, the more unconscious we are of it. We think we are doing what we want, but it is out of the fear of desire, because nothing is more fearful than desire, to get what we want, to do what we want. Phillips goes on to say: "Our perversions could be no problem except that often they are an attack on something else that we really want."[8]

So—to go back to the barred man of our example—what allows him to make a third choice, to move out of forbidden mirages to the fantasies of "unforbidden" pleasures? I think it might have to do with this example, with Oedipus, with time, with generational difference, with an authority that is protective, not forbidding, one that performs a non-sadistic paternal function. This is how our example goes:

> A little five-year-old girl is playing house with her mother. The little girl says: "My husband is an architect [her father is an architect] and I have four kids with him and I am a stay-at-home mom" [a slight jab at the mother, who is a heart surgeon and works a lot.]

The mother says: "Oh, how interesting, my husband is also an architect [probably a slightly revengeful jab back]." The little girl, confused, says: "Your husband is my husband, I want to marry Dad and have kids with him."

The mother, now feeling less vengeful and more amused, says: "I understand your wish; I also wanted to marry my dad, but Grandma told me that he is her husband and my father, and I only had to wait, wait, for my time would come to find a husband of my own, and look! I waited and found a great husband. You will get your turn, your time will come, you just have to wait."

The little girl listens attentively and says: "Ohhh-kaaay... but can he at least be an architect?"

It's perfect... the little girl, with the help of a protective authority, is finding her way to compromises made, unforbidden pleasures found, and the concepts of time and space.

I think this example encapsulates that patience is the key to working through the Oedipus complex. The little girl has to wait.

The "NO" in Oedipus is a protective *no*; it is not an authoritarian one. It has authority, but it is not dictatorial. Please, ladies and gentlemen of my geography, yes, there are moments when that geography is colored with its own specific shade of blue. In Iran, socio-politically we have never experienced an authority that is not authoritarian, but often, when the father says *no* to the son with regard to the possibility of incestuous sexual relations, he is inviting him to the land of "unforbidden" pleasures, towards the pleasure principle, and protecting him from the horrors of an incest actualized.

Here again: our Kantian barred hero is able to walk away from the deal: not even tempted, just thinking "How funny is this deal?" for somewhere along the way he has been introduced to the reality principle, has been narcissistically injured, has had to acknowledge generational difference, recognizes that pleasure is only pleasure that is delayed and diminished, otherwise it is a mirage, a ghost in the shadow of the death drive. He patiently walks away, finding the whole situation comical, as he bids farewell to the forbidders. He leaves the forbidders unemployed. Until the next choice, for they are formidable, these forbidders.

I also mentioned "love" in the context of the man of our example. Freud's famous quote on love: well, we are establishing that a narcissism untouched is at the core of melancholia, but such a limitation to narcissism knows only one barrier, love for oneself and love for others in the progress of mankind, just as in individual transformations. According to Freud in his paper on group psychology, "love alone acts as a civilizing factor, in the sense that it brings a change from egoism to altruism."[9]

Freud goes on to say:

[I]t is interesting to see that it is precisely those sexual impulses that are inhibited in their aims which achieve such lasting ties between people. But this can easily be understood from the fact that they are not capable of complete satisfaction, while sexual impulsions which are uninhibited in their aims suffer an extraordinary reduction through the discharge of energy every time the sexual aim is attained. It is the fate of sensual love to become extinguished when it is satisfied, for it to be able to last, it must from the beginning be mixed with purely affectionate components—with such, that is, as are inhibited in their aims—or it must itself undergo a transformation of this kind.[10]

So you see, our man from the Kantian example is bound to face an extraordinary disappointment, for the moment he satisfies his sexual aim with the supposed woman of his dreams he is bound to face the mirage that she is, a mirage of flesh and blood, for according to Lacan, whatever you think the "thing" will be, it will turn out to be a gift of shit.

The only thing that will derail this fate of sexual love is if it is colored with affection, with the reality principle, and with "unforbidden" pleasures. How to turn shit not into gold but into ordinary happiness, or common unhappiness, as Freud defined the goal of psychoanalysis: to move from "neurotic misery to common unhappiness"; common unhappiness is riddled with a variety of unforbidden pleasures. But in order to arrive there, you must first learn how to love.

Please excuse my digression from Forough; I am just attempting to practice diving. I don't want to use the sometimes un-sophisticated, reductionist language of psychoanalysis to say that her mother was overbearing, her father cruel. She was the third of seven children, and so on, and so on. The Forough whom I got to know over those few short weeks when she came to see me every afternoon from 3:00 to 3:50 was full of life, she was funny, she had the most contagious laugh, and she always kept flight in mind; just listen to this:

I feel blue,

I feel blue

I go to the porch and caress the stretched skin of the night with my fingers

I see that all lights of affinities are dark

No one to introduce me to the sun,

No one to take me to the gathering of doves.

Keep the flight in mind,

The bird is mortal.[11]

I Shall Hail the Sun Again

I shall hail the sun again

I shall hail the streamlet that flowed in me,

The clouds that were my lengthy thoughts,

The painful growth of aspens in the garden

Passing through the dry seasons with me,

The flock of crows that gifts me with

The fields' nocturnal scent,

And I hail my mother who lived in a mirror

And resembled me in my old age,

And I will hail again the earth, whose inflamed womb I filled

With the green seeds of my lust for repetition.

I Shall Hail the Sun Again.[12]

The Forough whom I got to know had many highs and lows. She had a fundamental discontent, *Unbehagen*, in a feminine sort of way, but she was full of life and curiosity; she wanted to devour life, discover things; she was ultimately quite political, and she became more and more political toward the end of her life. I thought this was a great sign for her; she was opening up, coming outside of herself, entering the outside world, and yet her most powerful prison guard was her punitive superego; she felt guilty of something and she needed to be punished for it, and this was repeated in her frequently sadomasochistic relationships.

Ultimately, she identified with a community of lepers. She told me she felt at home with them, mostly understood by them, so basically, she identified with what the rest of the world sees as a community of monsters who have to be isolated, so that they do not infect others. This is how Forough felt deep down: she felt she was a glorious leper.

She was extremely self-critical, in a narcissistic way, and these were the only times when she would become boring, for self-criticism at the end of the day is a defense against thinking about something deeper: it closes the discourse, it is joyless and beyond the pleasure principle. In an omnipotent, narcissistic way, everything was her fault; her work was never good enough. She was very aware that at some level adopting Hossein, the child of two lepers, had to do with her feelings of guilt about the abandonment of her own son, Kamyar, whom she affectionately called Kami. Logically, she knew that she had lost custody of Kami, but her unconscious believed otherwise, for guilt over Kami found its bed already made up with guilt(s) past, entangled in sheets of crime and punishment, *après-coup*.

The day of her death was preceded by a few unsuccessful suicide attempts and a period of psychiatric hospitalization. I came to know that she was a melancholic at heart who desperately attempted to move toward a successful mourning via her poetry. She oscillated between a Dostoyevsky and Duras kind of mourning, and melancholia; we can even see that in her poetry. Sometimes, even in the same poem, we see a clear struggle between life and death, between pleasure and beyond the pleasure principle. Forough was the kind of woman who is always in search of *jouissance*, of forbidden pleasures. Forough desperately—and at times successfully—tried to move from our bizarre, comical Kantian proposal, but ultimately such a dilemma was exactly what she ended up with on the last day of her life, given the choice: to die herself, or to allow a school bus full of children to die? Her fate on the day she died was very similar to that of our Kantian protagonist. Perhaps the repetition compulsion of her life was always between these two choices, without ever a third option. I find her short life to be a narrative of such a Kantian tragicomedy.

She chose death, becoming an example *par excellence* of it. Although it is indeed true that the death drive is connected to aggression and violence toward the other, this has been overemphasized in the literature, as it is merely a secondary established link. The death drive is always primarily toward oneself; it is a regression from object libido to primary narcissism: the death drive is a withdrawal within oneself. And this is why melancholia is always in the shadow of narcissism. This is André Green's death narcissism (or negative narcissism), for we cannot forget that we have life narcissism as well. And if—unjustly—I wanted to draw a one-line distinction between the two, I would say that life narcissism is inevitably diminished and delayed narcissism. I believe there is a clear quantitative factor to the distinction between life narcissism and death narcissism. It is not just a matter of a qualitative difference.

On the day of her death, Forough made an impossible choice for herself: one that was no choice at all, as is our Kantian example—an impossible choice, a no-choice, a repetition of a series of non-choices she had made from very early on in her life. On that day, Forough swerved her jeep to avoid an oncoming school bus and was thrown out of her car, saving the children, the child within herself, the child she gave birth to and the child of the lepers she adopted, believing in the beginning of a cold season, with only her voice remaining.

This "saving," this "survival," became feasible only with the gallows awaiting her at the end of the road.

The Captive

I want to leave but I know

I don't have the strength

Even if the warden agrees

I've lost the strength to fly away.

Every bright morning

Outside the cage

A child's gaze smiles at me

As I start a happy song

his kissing lips search for mine.

Oh sky, if I decide to fly away one day

From this silent jail,

What should I say to this child's crying eyes?

Let me be, I am a captive bird.[13]

Let Us Believe in the Beginning of a Cold Season

And this is me

A lonely woman

At the beginning of a cold season

At the beginning of earth's understanding of corruption

And the simple sad despair of the sky

And the impotence of these cemented hands.

Time passed,

Time passed and the clock chimed four times,

The clock chimed four times.

Today is the first day of winter,

I know the season's secret

And I do understand the moments

The savior is in his grave

And the earth, the generous earth,

Signifies peace

Time passed and the clock chimed four times

Perhaps the truth was those two young hands

Those two young hands buried under the continuous snowfall

And next year, when spring mates with the sky beyond the window, the outburst of the fountain of green stems on her body will blossom.

O my sweetheart

My one and only sweetheart.[14]

Notes

1 Freud, *Group Psychology and the Analysis of the Ego.*
2 Freud, *On the History of the Psycho-Analytic Movement, Papers on Metapsychology and Other Works*, 237–258; Farrokhzad, "The Bird May Die..." (my translation).
3 Lacan Online, "What Does Lacan Say about... Jouissance?"
4 Kant, *Kant: Critique of Pure Reason.*
5 Freud, *Beyond the Pleasure Principle.*
6 Žižek, *Žižek Reader.*
7 Phillips, *Unforbidden Pleasures.*
8 Phillips, *Unforbidden Pleasures.*
9 Freud, *Group Psychology and the Analysis of the Ego.*
10 Freud, *Group Psychology and the Analysis of the Ego.*
11 Farrokhzad, "The Bird May Die..." (my translation).
12 Farrokhzad, "Excerpts and Poems" (my translation).
13 Farrokhzad, "Excerpts and Poems" (my translation).
14 Farrokhzad, "Excerpts and Poems" (my translation).

L

L and I always meet for dinner, never for lunch, for the day always carries too much light for our heavy, dark conversations. She often jokes, laughing hysterically, that she feels suicidal after a dinner with me. L, oh L: I can just imagine her in all her slenderness and glamour. She is a nomad at heart, and this nomadism is always reflected in her fashion: she has a stunning face, but not in the clichéd sense of beauty: she has a combination of fragility and strength that is very hard to come by these days. People either love her or hate her, but indifference is not something she is even slightly familiar with, nor is it bestowed upon her. She is intense in everything she does, for good or for bad, but no one can say she is boring, and she is my darling friend.

Above all else, L despises the politically correct discourse of our times, and it is my professional clinical opinion that she is one of the most well-analyzed people I have ever known. This is an opinion most of my colleagues would not share, but that is because they have not gotten to love L over the years. The truth is that most of the people I love, desire, and enjoy would be excluded from the normative well-analyzed club, but that just might be saying something about my state of mind, which is a whole other palette of the Blues, *chiaroscuro*, to be fair...

L has been in four-times-weekly analysis in Boston for ten years with an analyst I deeply respect; she still not only idealizes her analyst in the most glorious of ways, but her love for her analyst has led our brilliant L to develop the most sophisticated arguments in defense of "idealization" against everyone who pathologizes this position, or criticizes L's analyst for not having worked through this idealization with her.

Once I was careless enough to get into an intellectual discussion with L, saying something along the lines of: But idealization, just like identification, is always ambivalent at heart, my dear friend... And she, being the curious and vivacious L that she is, asked me to tell her more about identification according to Freud, but there was hurt in her voice. I went on quoting Freud's paper on group psychology:

DOI: 10.4324/9781003269113-14

...identification can turn into an expression of tenderness as easily as into a wish for someone's removal. It behaves like a derivative of the first oral phase of the organization of the libido, in which the object that we long for and prize is assimilated by the eating and in that way annihilates as such. The cannibal, as we know, has remained at this standpoint; he has a devouring affection for his enemies and only devours people of whom he is fond.

I felt that I had wounded my friend with all these theories.
  L said:

Not you too... really, do you think I did not see him that day in New York, unable to catch a taxi? Do you think I am blind to how he mixes hours and appointments? He has really held on to the Freudian notion that there is no time in the unconscious... Gohar, come on, you know me better than that... remember when I told you about his favorite interpretation, the one he repeats with such pride that every time it seems he had the idea for the first time... and I pretend that it is the first time I am hearing it, because I love him.

I choose to idealize him because he has been a thoughtful and helpful analyst, and he has done his very best. It's not even melodramatic, like, he has not saved my life, I was not dying... he has not shown me the path towards enlightenment and he has definitely not shown me the light, our path has gotten darker and darker, just like my dinners with you... but my analyst and I laugh together more and more as time goes by... again, just like our dinners.

We have found pleasure in each other's company... and when, time after time, I would go in with my repetitive obsessive stories with hysterical spice... he would listen every time, probably pretending in turn that it was the first time I was verbalizing such a scenario, as God knows, the actors changed but the plot remained the same! It is still the same even after ten years of being with my idealized analyst, but really not quite the same... Funny, I think people who claim they do not idealize their analysts have extremely idealized ideas about what their analysis has done for them. I just love my analyst, I love this ordinarily exceptional man who has been a witness to the story of my life.

Once I asked L why she did not become an analyst. She responded:

But I am not a humanitarian, I am not interested in helping other people, I am just interested in doing interesting things. It is boredom that is the fundamental sin, which as you know is quite different to the capacity to be alone. I loved it when Donald Winnicott elaborated that the capacity to be alone is clearly not withdrawal or loneliness, seeing it develop out of the child's internalization of the non-intrusive presence of a mothering figure.

I say that I always thought of it as the internalization of a maternal figure who can be present while the child plays alone: a kind of opposite to André Green's "dead mother," where the mother is present, definitely not dead, but consumed by melancholia, and therefore completely emotionally unavailable to the child, even though she is right there. A mother who was once libidinally cathected to her child, but out of a bereavement of her own has completely decathected from her child, and taken all that extra libido to a primary narcissism of her own, back to her own ego.

L says: "Oh, stop, please, do you see why I become suicidal after a dinner with you?" We laugh, we both laugh together, moving on from these theories to the beauty of her necklace.

L was unquestionably the one who hurriedly joined me on my welcoming bathroom floor after my father died. I did not want to see or talk to anyone, not even her. Any time that somebody said "I am sorry for your loss," or offered condolences, I would get so angry... as if they were becoming agents of the very reality I was trying to deny, almost like a psychotic. For introducing reality to psychotics, in my opinion, is even crueler than giving them shock therapy; the real shock is reality... But L, her usual impressive self, refused to listen to me and would just come in and sit next to me, like the best of analysts. She never said "I am sorry for your loss." She was just there. Sometimes she said something really funny, like "Dr. Homayounpour, boy, you have hit rock bottom, haven't you? If only your patients could see you now!" and somehow that would make me laugh... at other times she would let me be angry at her, and just once she said: "You know, I lost my father when I was nine years old, and I survived. You will too, you are stronger than you think..." Somehow, in a way that goes beyond the empathy that is in fashion these days, that really helped. It is as if the thought had not crossed my mind that people survive, I was so narcissistically wounded that I had become oblivious to the world outside of me, and in her own way she brought me back to the world of objects, outside of my protective narcissistic shell.

Another time she asked me a theoretical psychoanalytic question and suddenly my eyes were shining, and I went into elaborate explanations of obsessions; later on she told me that her question was not a trick to inject a dose of life into me, she was just curious about obsessions, and she finds it playfully amusing and enjoyable to watch me eroticize such theories.

Then one day she said: "Enough is enough. Get up, go to work, your patients need you." I said I thought you were not a humanitarian... she said: "I am not. I am just on the side of life." So, I said, I will have a baby... She said: "Brilliant idea, but this one is out of my hands, so get up, eat and you can still wear your father's shirt." That whole time I was wearing his blue cotton shirt that he was wearing last on his tiny little boat...

My husband said "Leave her alone, she will vacate her bathroom whenever she is ready," and in the meantime he had transformed my bathroom into a lovely place, with flowers and beautiful towels and soaps that smelled like jasmine, *Yasmin* in Farsi. *Yasmin* is my Proustian madeleine, for smell can be as powerful as taste for our psyches, if not more powerful. The smell of *Yasmin* for me is associated with my father, with my paternal grandmother, Gohar Taj, and with Shiraz, my father's motherland. These little white flowers are also aptly called "poet's jasmine"; the masterly Bengali poet Rabindranath Tagore has a poem that comes to my mind as I write these lines— "The First Jasmines":

Ah, these jasmines, these white jasmines!

I seem to remember the first day when I filled my hands with these jasmines, these white jasmines.

I have loved the sunlight, the sky and the green earth;

I have heard the liquid murmur of the river through the darkness of midnight;

Autumn sunsets have come to me at the bend of a road in the

lonely waste, like a bride raising her veil to accept her lover.

Yet my memory is still sweet with the first white jasmines

that I held in my hands when I was a child.

Many a glad day has come in my life, and I have laughed with

merrymakers on festival nights.

On grey mornings of rain I have crooned many an idle song.

I have worn round my neck the evening wreath of bakulas woven by the hand of love.

Yet my heart is sweet with the memory of the first fresh

jasmines that filled my hands when I was a child.[1]

I am reminded of that spring day when my father picked me up from the airport in Shiraz carrying jasmine he had gathered in a small white cotton bag to greet me upon my arrival. All I remember from that trip of many years ago is that when we got into a taxi from the airport my father got into a whole discussion with the driver about Sartre's existentialism. As I listened, I kept smelling my jasmine. My father took everyone seriously, and at heart, until the very end, he remained faithful to his leadership and pioneering position in the spirit of adult literacy. Education remained the foremost significant thing in life and a human right; he believed that everybody should have access to education, and that it was never too late to learn.

Once on a plane he began a loud lecture, much to the surprise of the Air France flight crew, declaring that he understood if the food, the chairs, and the service were better in business class, but what was absolutely unacceptable was that newspapers were being denied to the economy passengers: that was unfathomable.

My repeated airport and airplane associations when it comes to my life, and especially to my father, do not escape me and yet another very clear and painful airport dream is imposing itself on me. It wants to reveal itself. As hard as I have tried to repress this dream that I had three years after I lost my father, it comes back with full force, imposing itself on my preconscious and eventually landing in the album of my memories.

But this is not a dream, this is the story of what really happened while I was in transit at some strange airport somewhere in the world, where the reality principle momentarily abandoned me. I saw a man who looked exactly like my father from behind. He was wearing the exact kind of hat you used to wear, one that I did not like, not finding it contemporary enough, but at that moment the sight of that hat, with your favorite khaki signature jacket, the man was wearing a crisp white shirt as you always did—heaven knows you had too many white shirts, all exactly the same—and he walked with your posture, your very specific posture.

I started following him, in tears, convinced that I had re-found you in that unfamiliar airport. I ran after you, taking every turn you took, having lost any concepts of time and space. I had to be at my gate on the other side of the airport in fifty minutes, but none of the derivatives of the reality principle were available to me, I just ran after you, convinced that we had re-found each other in transit. The moment you slowed down at a gate, I hesitantly slowed down, as if there was maybe a slight part of me that was still in touch with the outside world and knew full well that the moment the man turned around, any possibility of finding you right there would evaporate... so I just wanted to follow you at a pace that would never allow me to reach you, so that I could go on dreaming, so that I would not have to wake up, so that my dream would not turn into a nightmare,... but you slowed down at your gate, and in lieu of my best efforts not to see your face, you turned around and slapped me with that unfamiliar gaze. There was nothing even remotely familiar about this stranger, absolutely nothing that resembled you... the moment he turned around I looked at my watch and started running to my own gate...

I have a patient who brings me jasmine once a year; she is from Shiraz. I don't analyze it, as sometimes white jasmine is just white jasmine, a gift from the stars.

Note

1 Tagore, "The First Jasmines," in *Gitanjali* (translated by author).

Beyond "Locality"

The Voyage of the Shitty Pebble

I would like to begin with a play on free association; what comes to mind when one is confronted with "locality"? Is it trans-locality, is it beyond global? Is it the politics of globalization, a critique of the political economy, and deconstructionism?

Well, certainly, these and many more intriguing words might come to the minds of many of our intellectual friends.

My own associations take me back a few years to when I saw a cartoon strip in *"Libération,"* illustrated by Riad Sattouf, a French-Syrian cartoonist, a cartoon which struck me with its obvious yet forgotten message: the cartoon was about a Syrian village school without toilets.[1] Kids had to do their stool around the school and wipe themselves on the pebbles, and as time passed, the circle of shit and shitty pebbles began to get larger and larger, and further and further away from the village.

Cities were taken over by the nauseating smell of shit, and no one really knew where it was coming from. One day one of the schoolboys, now a teenager, who was fed up with the shitty situation, decided to travel to the seaside in France. Upon his arrival in France he heard people complaining about shitty pebbles being all around them. Pensively, he exclaimed: "Shit travels…"

Today, Sattouf's illustration seems almost prophetic.

***

Attempting to go beyond the simplifying seduction of binaries, of local versus global. Especially in recent years, it seems that there has been an eroticization of the "local," in its various forms of productions. Locality, it seems, has become a product, a commodity in its own accord, capitalism's newest ideological bestseller, and here we are staying faithful to Marx's assertion that commodity is the ultimate object of fetish.[2] Here we are clearly in Žižek territory: he tells us that we buy our overpriced cup of Starbucks coffee, but feel less guilty knowing that a small portion of the proceeds will go to hungry African children.[3]

DOI: 10.4324/9781003269113-15

As I was thinking about writing this piece, I was on a plane, where I found the August issue of the magazine *Wallpaper* next to my seat, and, alas, as I flipped through the pages, this is what found me:

"Turkish delight, Ali robe and towel set, by DAY studio and Frette."[4]

It was indeed a delightful advertisement showcasing the loveliest designs by the Istanbul-based firm DAY studio, a design which fuses the shape of a traditional Kaftan with the lightness and patterns of a *peshtemal* (Turkish bath towel), inspired by local manufacturing techniques and craftsmen, in collaboration with the Italian powerhouse of Frette.

Eroticizing locality can be dangerous; it can alienate and isolate thoughts and cultures, and for a while it can provide the illusion that what is home-grown—i.e., the shitty pebble—will stay home-grown.

But what is really home-grown, and in complete isolation from the rest of the world, in any case?

Some would say Persian and Turkish delights, but I am not convinced. I am, however, convinced that we need to move away from this politics of naming and sameness toward a subversive discourse of difference.

Maybe we have made locality a new modern erotic, a modern defense to deny the arrival of the shitty pebble. Well, here we are dealing with the return of the repressed; our defenses have been violently taken away and the shitty pebbles are here, and here to stay. So let us make an attempt to analyze them, to transform them beyond a politics of locality.

Maybe it is as Žižek says: that after every attempt at a leftist revolution, we have to face a Nazi uprising. Could locality be the Nazi uprising to a genuine global revolutionary attempt that was due to the age of cyberspace, since borders between where people were located became blurred: for a while "internet domains" did not have a country code, but this has clearly changed.

The modern subject is a dislocated subject, and this is not such a bad thing: within this dis-location there are intimate possibilities of becomings, but there are dangers, too… we might become completely lost, depressed, manic, schizophrenic, or ultimately desireless.

This is not merely a pessimistic view: it is an active pessimist's view, since it is exactly at the moment of the return of the repressed that it becomes possible to face our unconscious in a way that will lead to freedom and sublimation at the edge of the language, to have the courage to face what we knew all along but did not want to remember.

We do indeed have a sadomasochistic relationship to memory.

It is Diderot's *Jacques the Fatalist* and his master's dislocation that, I believe, holds the potential to open up the possibilities of what I would like to term a nomadic becoming: a becoming that changes with seasons, transient, never fixed.

Let us adhere to Diderot's *Jacques the Fatalist* and his master's conceptualization of "beyond locality."

"How did the two meet? Incidentally, like everybody else, what were their names? None of your business; where did they come from? Somewhere close by; where do they go to? Do we ever Know where we go?"[5]

Locality is only a "chimera" to divide us and "put us in our place," so to speak. I propose a rebellion aimed towards the limit of placing, categorizing, naming, and localizing. This does not mean that we cannot have geographies of locality, emphasizing difference rather than sameness. For it is a politics of difference, one comprised of a nomadic identity, I am proposing, not one that is a relativist and parochial *zeitgeist*.

I do not adhere to locality; it exists solely at the level of imagination… the imagination of those called local by the Other and, of course, the imagination of the Other when thinking about the local. And they are both playing this "name game" to keep their unconscious pact.

Well, it is too late: the sleeping dogs (who were never really sleeping, according to Freud) are now wide awake, and barking loud and clear.[6]

We have entered the era of the return of the repressed.

We cannot count on "locality," but we can be certain that shitty pebbles are traveling our way as we speak, so put on your Ali robe-and-towel set: you will need it.

Notes

1 Sattouf, *Les Cailloux Merdeux*.
2 Marx and Mandel, *Capital: Critique of Political Economy, Volume 1*.
3 Žižek, "Fat-Free Chocolate and Absolutely No Smoking: Why Our Guilt about Consumption Is All-Consuming."
4 Wallpaper*, "Handmade 2016: Hotel Wallpaper*."
5 Diderot, *Jacques le Fataliste* (my translation from the French).
6 Freud, "Analysis Terminable and Interminable (1937)."

Narcissism Becomes a Hazard to Our "Building a Boat"

Béla Grunberger, an almost forgotten psychoanalyst and, in my opinion, the master of understanding narcissism, writes:

> We have seen how importantly the trauma of the loss of narcissistic omnipotence figures in the development of the child. We have also seen that, although he represses this trauma, the child nevertheless keeps a bitter memory of this affront and will seek to redress it, to cancel it out. One could regard all the manifestations of civilizations as a kaleidoscope of different attempts by man to restore narcissistic omnipotence. Neurosis often being an unsuccessful one.[2]

So neurosis, it seems, is an attempt to rebuff our narcissistic injury to our omnipotence: "Paradoxically, passivity offers protection against the danger of narcissistic trauma: 'If I turn over the initiative to others, I cannot be painfully surprised by discovery of my own impotence'."[3]

In "Mourning and Melancholia" Freud elaborates that there is a direct correlation between those who become melancholics and their narcissistic object-choice. Hence melancholia borrows certain of its attributes from mourning, and the others from the process of regression from narcissistic object-choice to narcissism.

In some ways melancholia is like mourning, "a reaction to the real loss of a loved object," but it is differently determined:

> The loss of a love-object is an excellent opportunity for the ambivalence in love-relationships to make itself effective and come into the open. Where there is a disposition to obsessional neurosis the conflict due to ambivalence gives a pathological cast to mourning and forces it to express itself in the form of self-reproaches to the effect that the mourner himself is to blame for the loss of the loved object, i.e. that he has willed it.[4]

Freud brings the obsessions that can develop out of melancholia back to loss, through death but also after a person has been slighted or neglected, showing

DOI: 10.4324/9781003269113-16

that "opposed feelings of love and hate" can come just as much from rejection as from loss. That "hate," mixed with love, might result in an abasement of the original love, and hence to a "sadistic satisfaction from its suffering." Other results of such suffering include the patient "taking revenge on the original object and in tormenting their loved one through their illness, having resorted to it in order to avoid the need to express their hostility to him openly." Indeed, rather than loss, this may be a suffering in the patient occasioned by someone still to be found close by. "The melancholic's erotic cathexis in regard to his object has thus undergone a double vicissitude," explains Freud; "part of it has regressed to identification, but the other part, under the influence of the conflict due to ambivalence, has been carried back to the stage of sadism, which is nearer to that conflict."

> It is this sadism alone that solves the riddle of the tendency to suicide which makes melancholia so interesting—and so dangerous.

These strong reactions, according to Freud, come back to "the ego's self-love, which we have come to recognize as the primal state from which instinctual life proceeds"; in an extreme case, melancholia is the means by which the "ego can consent to its own destruction":

> We have long known, it is true, that no neurotic harbours thoughts of suicide which he has not turned back upon himself from murderous impulses against others, but we have never been able to explain what interplay of forces can carry such a purpose through to execution. The analysis of melancholia now shows that the ego can kill itself only if, owing to the return of the object-cathexis, it can treat itself as an object— if it is able to direct against itself the hostility which relates to an object and which represents the ego's original reaction to objects in the external world. Thus in regression from narcissistic object-choice the object has, it is true, been got rid of, but it has nevertheless proved more powerful than the ego itself. In the two opposed situations of being most intensely in love and of suicide the ego is overwhelmed by the object, though in totally different ways.

I remember a day at a very prestigious psychoanalytic congress when the speaker went on and on, analyzing a dream of her own in which the famous late French psychoanalyst André Green had come to her, telling her that she was the chosen one for him to carry his legacy and further elaborate his theories. We know that according to Freud, the language of dreams is the language of wish fulfillments, where our repressed unconscious desires attempt to find satisfaction, and to resolve some conflict between a want and a prohibition. In other words, the wish lingers on the very thing that has been forbidden. It seems that we keep coming back to the forbidden and the forbidders...

My dear friend G was sitting next to me and we both looked at each other, in that familiar way you share within an intimacy that is rare to come by. I said: She's so lucky, wow... my dreams are full of shit, guilt, conflict, and pain; she belongs to a more advanced species.

G, smiling, said:

> I am in your camp, my dear, the underdeveloped... you know I had a dream last night that the toilet was not working in my flat and I was getting more and more anxious, thinking that all the shit would rise up and take over the place, and I was obsessed with collecting all the toilet paper I could find, rolls and rolls of it, but the more I collected, the more anxious I became, and suddenly I woke up... How I wish that André Green had a made a visit; I am sure that would have sustained my dream work.

At this exact moment of G's and my joyous collusion, an alliance that was secretly quite narcissistic at that moment, at this instant of judging, my psychic apparatus would not let me "get away with it," forcing me to remember my own Milan Kundera dream I wrote about many years ago in *Doing Psychoanalysis in Tehran*: yet another not-so-friendly reminder that we are all everything. As such, allow me to take this opportune moment to profess that if there is anywhere throughout my associations in *Persian Blues* where I have come close to judging, I ask the reader to take it with a grain of salt, a drop of salt water. It is merely indicative of a shade of blue that I have not fully integrated into my subjectivity yet; palettes of the Blues which are still in search of becomings.

But I do not forbid this pleasurable narcissistic twinkle, and I say: "It would have been absolutely delightful if Green gave you a session in the middle of your shit dream" ... *shh, shh*, the noises from behind were asking us primitive people to be quiet... so like two mischievous kids in elementary school we started writing notes to each other, and I felt this immense pleasure that we were in each other's un-sophisticated camp, he and I.

In this short story by Lydia Davis, what touches the reader, what makes it a brilliant story, is her playfulness with narcissism, for indeed playful narcissism is always diminished narcissism:

On the Train

First sequence: feeling of closeness to a total stranger only by sharing the disgust of watching two women talking loudly; she declares, bad manners.

Second sequence, later on: the stranger is picking his nose and she is dripping tomato sauce on her newspaper; she declares, bad habits.

The following declaration/confession; most sincere and utterly objective, with grave consequences: she wouldn't report this if she was the one picking her nose.

The finale, with two different frames: the stranger still picking his nose; a perfect image of those women reading, in perfect harmony. She declares: blamelessness.[5]

A genius I loved and greatly admired who had become an international superstar used to tell me: "You know I became a genius after I became famous!" What a wonderful joke on narcissism, what a delightful awareness of it.

André Green (who, unfortunately, has never visited me in my dreams, although I have tried to invite him time after time), as I have already mentioned, makes a significant distinction between life (positive) narcissism and death (negative) narcissism. Death narcissism is the withdrawal of libido from objects, from the outside world, precisely as Freud discusses the dynamics of melancholia; it is the dis-objectilizing function of the drive. In my own words, it is a resistance to difference, to absence, and to moving from need to desire. It is an ego overwhelmed and split by a hypercathesis of libido, spilling into the derivatives of the death drive, to beyond the pleasure principle. A resistance to remembering what we already know. Life narcissism is creativity, sublimation, and ambition, it is necessary to survive, it is our survival instinct, it is how we begin to eroticize our bodies and start to have an image of their cohesiveness, illusory as that might be, but a necessary illusion, part and parcel of the neurotic structure.

Notes

1 Davis, "Five Short Stories—Lydia Davis."
2 Grunberger, *Narcissism: Psychoanalytic Essays.*
3 Grunberger, *Narcissism: Psychoanalytic Essays.*
4 Freud, "Mourning and Melancholia," 237–258.
5 Davis, "Five Short Stories—Lydia Davis."

Inflation / Inflated Blues

The day is 1 August 2018. The Iranian currency has lost eighty per cent of its value, the country is on the verge of complete bankruptcy and in meltdown, everything we owned has been reduced to nothing. Money is assuming its rightful place as just paper, all symbolic meaning is being sucked out of it… what a strange phase. I have been oscillating between sadness and anger since the beginning of the Trump administration; it is so seductive for me to get emotionally involved, especially after the "Muslim ban." This temptation arises when Iranians are separated from their children, or when a patient reports on the couch: "I have just gotten my visa approved to take my thir-teen-year-old daughter to New York for cancer treatment; you know, Doctor, this is how terrorists are made," or with the thoughts of the shattered hopes of dispossessed refugees and so many others affected by Trump's new policies.

But I must attempt to retain my analytic attitude, futile as that attempt may be.

Didn't Trump get democratically elected? Didn't millions of people in the United States vote for him? Did he not say exactly what his plans were for America? Did he not say specifically that he would implement a Muslim ban, anti-immigration, and anti-refugee policies? Did he not say that he would build a wall? People kept saying it was just campaign rhetoric.

Is this not reminiscent of Hitler? For God's sake, he wrote a book saying exactly what he was going to do, discussing his worldview in detail. People still voted for him in large numbers.

As a psychoanalyst, I think it is important to sometimes shift our attention from Trump himself to the Trump phenomenon. This dialectic will include the people who voted for him.

Is it a coincidence that the Trump phenomenon was preceded by two terms of the Obama presidency? Obama, the quintessential politician of this century?

Is it not bizarre that some of the same people who voted for Obama voted for Trump?!

Is it an accident that Trump won because Hillary Clinton was the one running against him? Is America still more sexist than racist? Not that I am a

DOI: 10.4324/9781003269113-17

fully fledged Hillary fan, by any means... I wonder if there is still a stronger negative reaction to women in positions of power. Hillary fainted, and the world panicked: this indicated that she might be too weak to be a leader; but she was also deeply hated by both men and women for being too phallic.

It was a lose–lose situation for Hillary; she did not have a chance, and anyone who ran against her would have won, even Trump—or especially Trump. I say especially Trump perhaps because he represents the lost narcissism of America, hence the slogan "Make America Great Again" from a macho, rich, woman-grabbing, impulsive bully, who gets what he wants when he wants it.

It could be that people voted for Trump because they have a strong wish to resurrect the lost paternal function of today's world. They want a rich daddy to stand up for them; they crave it, they need it... but ah, they do not know that he is just a mirage in the desert, an absolute *Sarab*, as we say in my mother-tongue...

Trump is the return of the repressed, the uncanny return of that which is strangely, unbearably familiar, and this could be why people voted for him in the secret ballot. They were unaware of why, but they were attracted to him like a butterfly to the candle, like the needle of the Sleeping Beauty, cursed, destined by the evil of the dark side. But the dark will only become "speakable" when we look into our mirrors and find our own dark shadows, and grant them visas to come in. Otherwise they will haunt us in the Oval Office when we don't even know why, when, and how we voted for Trump: hypnotized, following a part of ourselves we are so repelled with that it has come back to haunt us as the Trump phenomenon.

Paris Blues, or, Are You Going Home?

When everybody was leaving the country in the early years of the Islamic revolution, in the midst of all the disturbances and uncertain changes, we decided to leave Paris and the magical smell of Parisian *boulangeries*, my beloved kindergarten, and my best friend Lisa. This would become part of my repetition-compulsion to make moves against the tide for good or for bad: to swim upstream, so to speak. Years after our move from Paris, I decided to move to Tehran from Boston after years of my comfortable North American life, exactly when Ahmadinejad was elected president in Iran. Everybody around me looked question marks at me... well, they did not know that "disturbance" has accompanied me since I was very young, and that disturbance and I were intimate... disturbance has been my best friend and foe all my life: never boring, never without intensity, always subversive, eternally against the status quo... on the move, but with pain, loss, struggle, and with a particular fidelity to the different palettes of the Blues.

How bizarre it all felt when a classmate of mine at Queen's University in Canada asked: "Are you going home for the weekend?" She went on: "I am, it's twenty minutes away, and it's the only home I have ever known since I was born." I felt a combination of jealousy and sadness for her; maybe this sadness was a way of not seeing how sad her question made me feel. Are you going home? Where the hell is home? Home for me is associated with images of airports, boxes, and suitcases. I have the strangest relationship with Paris, the symbol of the Paradise Lost of my childhood, of fusions and pastries and my delicate mother and strong father. Somewhere along the way her delicacy turned to fragility and my father lost his joyful strength, moving toward various shades of the Blues.

Because there is a big difference between delicacy and fragility; delicacy is not frightened but the fragile gaze is always an anxious one.

With Paris I am like a wounded lover. Undesirable to get there again, but Paris is my first love.

I can't quite give up re-finding particular loved/flawed pieces of it.

DOI: 10.4324/9781003269113-18

In Niz Bogzared, This Too Shall Pass

This is precisely the antidote to trauma; nothing is that traumatic when you know it has a beginning and an end. Is this not why cutters give a physicality (an embodiment) to their pain? A beginning and an end, while giving it an architectural form, somehow makes it bearable, comprehensible. This is what we see with depression and melancholia: it is the certainty of the melancholic that this shall never ever pass that makes their depression so traumatizing and troubling. The timelessness of it all. This is also what makes melancholia so boring to listen to. The concreteness of it all, the masturbatory pleasures of a primary narcissism.

As soon as our melancholic finds a hole to the outside world, no matter how minuscule or how brief, the moment she pulls her head out of the snow... this death narcissism will have a chance to be transformed, as Charlotte Forten, one of the pioneers of the Blues genre from Pennsylvania, wrote in her diary after overcoming her depression in 1862: the songs "can't be sung without a full heart and a troubled spirit."[1]

Or when one thinks of the first publication of Blues sheet music, "I Got the Blues," published by the New Orleans musician Antonio Maggio in 1908, which is described as the first composition to link the condition of having the blues to the musical form that would become known as the "Blues." Some argue that it is the first publication of the 12-bar Blues, not the first Blues music ever. For the lyrics of early traditional Blues verses probably often consisted of a single line repeated four times. It was only in the first decades of the twentieth century that the most common current structure became standard: the so-called "AAB" pattern, consisting of a line sung over the first four bars, its repetition over the next four, and then a longer concluding line over the last bars.

It is to this AAB pattern that I have attempted to stay faithful in this book, and although our Blues gained an association with melancholia, it was never without humor, pleasure, and the possibilities of going beyond.

Inherent within the lyrics there is a clear possibility of a beyond to the "Blues," and it is humorous, and never boring.

DOI: 10.4324/9781003269113-19

Boredom is violent, it is actually a diagnostic tool for me with my patients: the moment an analysand and I laugh together at very dark shades of the blues, we both know that this too shall pass. That time and space have suddenly been introduced to our discourse.

Referring to the metaphor of a clowning mother, a mother trying to play the clown role for the infant to turn her cry and suffering into laughter, Christopher Bollas indicates that this clowning mother, through becoming internalized in the growing process of the infant, acts as a safeguard against fears of breakdown by instilling laughter, feelings of joy, and integration.[2] Alessandra Lemma highlights such an interaction as a kind of transformation in the interaction between mother and infant.[3] What is indigestible for the infant gets processed by the mother. Thus, these early experiences of shared laughter at the edge of bearable excitement, and the internalization of a mother/infant, help to digest these potentially destabilizing states and provide the infant with an internal sense of health and security against breakdown; Bollas calls this "cracking up together." The moment a melancholic patient and I crack up together, I know we have started the process of building our boat together; our cracking up together becomes an antidote to the patient cracking.

Lemma expresses that failed jokes are like a mother who has a disturbed capacity in interaction in its specific time and does not function very well as a clowning mother. Timing is everything in joke telling; it is exactly like giving an interpretation in the psychoanalytic session.

As I write these lines, I cannot help but think of Jacqueline Rose again. So it seems that mothers don't have to be just all loving, pure, and asexual, and conflictlessly adore their maternal role and duties, while breastfeeding their babies to be natural at any cost; we have to be funny too.

And yet I have found that both with adult patients and kids it is really helpful to be funny; some of the most effective moments I have experienced in analysis on both sides of the couch have been funny, humorous moments. Maybe if we really understood Freud's *Jokes and their Relation to the Unconscious* we would find our clue to why humor is such a helpful psychic tool toward building one's boat.[4] It is not that being funny and humorous is an added demand of purity loaded onto the shoulders of mothers, it is that for a joke to work you really have to be ok with being bad, sexual and aggressive. You have to have the key to open the floodgates to the return of the repressed, and we know very well that there is nothing pure or good in the land of the repressed.

Freud believed that a joke is an expression of the forbidden sexual and aggressive impulses which he already recognized as forming the latent content of dreams: an expression of obscenity and shamelessness, while accessing and celebrating an old infantile pleasure in the nonsensical.

Except that unlike dreams, jokes are a social phenomenon: humans are the only species capable of laughing and making each other laugh. It is a far cry from the narcissism of melancholia: for a joke to work there is the *a priori* assumption of the separateness and uniqueness of the other's mind. Narcissists can never tell a good joke; their jokes fail, so to speak. So the moment our melancholic character enters the realm of jokes, laughter and humor, he has certainly managed to—at least partially—break down the stone wall of narcissism.

Freud believed that the hedonistic factor of jokes is caused by the pleasure of saving psychic energy: through bypassing internal and external censors, sentiments that are felt to be dangerous, such as hostility, aggression, and sexuality are expressed and naturally result in pleasure. So in jokes we retrieve the infantile pleasures that have been lost to us as a result of the repressive forces of civilization; via a joke and the preconscious, we retrieve pleasures that were once lost.

In a fascinating essay by Vamik Volkan, sharing jokes becomes one of the first social responses given to mass trauma.[5] At first sight, sharing jokes during and after traumas seems like an irrational endeavor; but on a closer look, sharing jokes can become part of bereavement and mourning processes, and a defense against affects of a mass trauma, as well as an attempt to work through that very trauma. Lacan also recognizes the joke as an important aspect of an individual's growing capacity which addresses instilled limitations in the society, morality, and horror of the subject from the real order. Slavoj Žižek believes that comedy is a powerful way to symbolize a part of human experience which has silently frightened one's mind.

Volkan goes on elaborating regarding jokes in the heart of mass traumas, saying that one of the important distinctive factors is whether this trauma has broken the texture of the society in question or not. If the jokes coming after a trauma are in connection with lost people and things of the same society, generally it can be said that the spinal cord of the society has not been broken. On the other hand, when a mass trauma is inflicted by an Other's hands, the social texture of the victim group breaks, and common jokes concentrate more directly on its shame, its sense of humility and the threat directed at the group's identity. Then such jokes no longer function towards a constructive mourning process; they are practiced in order to lower the external hostile danger and to deny a sense of humility; hence they are much more on the defensive side.

As such, can we go as far as to say that jokes are the ultimate revolutionary acts, vehicles of uprising against oppression of the social fabric and the repression of our psychic apparatus?

In Iran, over the years, I have been astonished at the number of immensely funny jokes people make in extremely harsh, challenging, and traumatic situations. I have always felt that this is indeed not a society with a broken *spine* but one that continuously finds ways to elaborate, transform, represent, and, *alla fine*, to do it with a great deal of humor and desire for the pleasure principle via the playfulness of language.

And here is Freud again:

> For jokes do not, like dreams, create compromises; they do not evade the inhibition, but they insist on maintaining play with words or with nonsense unaltered. They restrict themselves, however, to a choice of occasions in which this play or this nonsense can at the same time appear allowable (in jests) or sensible (in jokes), thanks to the ambiguity of words and the multiplicity of conceptual relations. Nothing distinguishes jokes more clearly from all other psychical structures than this double-sidedness and this duplicity in speech. From this point of view at least the authorities come closest to an understanding of the nature of jokes when they lay stress on "sense in nonsense."[6]

In 1927 Freud recognized "jokes" as a potential wealth; an artificial process and a means for every individual to overcome the inevitable limits of life, sufferings and external reality. The ability to tell a joke is in the magical realm of play and metaphor, the antithesis of the psychic functioning of the melancholic.

***

Once a patient cried for the whole session, and I did not feel sad at all; I felt irritated and angry; I felt that her laments were covering up some aggression. I actually felt it could be a defense against the Blues; I found myself desperate for some genuine shade of the actual blues to emerge.

On another occasion a patient said: "You know, Doctor, what I fear the most about threesomes: I am convinced I will be the one completely ignored, a third wheel, so to speak, to their lovemaking..." I found myself very sad for the patient: all the connotation of Oedipal rivalry, primal scene, the voyeurism of it all... there was a deep sense of exclusion and rejection reminiscent of primal scenes and of an Oedipus not worked through that made my patient deeply sad; certainly one could hear echoes of this wished-for rejection as well. For deep down, no one really wants an Oedipal victory: nothing could be as dangerous, as horrifying.

The patient was clearly attempting to work through something, with continuous references to real and imagined offers of threesomes. I humorously wondered with her: it's quite incredible how many threesomes you get invited to. She replied: "They invite me in order to ignore me over and over again."

An obsessive patient was discussing his fears of flying and how it interferes with his work, which requires frequent flying; he feels as if he had no actual knowledge of the workings of airplanes, and therefore feels no control, and this makes his life desperate, quite wretched: as such he is terrified of falling into a deep depression. I said to him: Well, the solution seems to be clear, you need to become a pilot and pilot your own planes. That made him laugh...

Yet another patient told me about feeling so humiliated when her father, due to addiction struggles, had to sell her bedroom furniture, which my patient, as a thirteen-year-old adolescent, was so proud of owning. He sold it to her best friend's parents, so now every time she went to her best friend's house she would be confronted with a deep sense of loss and humiliation, while her oblivious best friend would show off her new bedroom suite to all their common friends. This made me deeply, deeply sad for my patient.

Mr. O, a fifty-year-old man, told me one day in his session that when he is about to leave his eighty-five-year-old mother's house, the mother cries every time like a little baby after her son, begging him to stay a bit longer. Eventually, upon his departure to his own home, which is just across town, she says: "At least call me when you get home so that I can be assured that you have safely arrived." When he calls from his home upon arrival, his sister picks up the phone and says: "But Mom fell asleep the moment you left." This is a mother who is incapable of holding her son in her mind; it is solely via the close, literal physicality of the son that he exists for her, giving a whole new definition to out of sight, out of mind. This made me immensely sad for him. This is the idea that object is need and need is object, for you have to be connected to something in order not to feel a pathological adhesiveness to it; there has to come a point where the object is not purely need; that will be possible only if the mother can keep her child in her mind, and once you have secured your place in her mind, you can move toward the outside, outside of each other, doing cartwheels and all, for as one Blues song goes: "One cannot lose a thing if one belongs to it."

This is also where psychoanalytic ethics comes from—it can come only from a subject: in other words, from a sense of separateness, of a distance between I and the other...

Hence ethics comes from a seduction that was not actualized, from longing, all the various possibilities when need and object are not the same anymore.

Ethics comes from seeing the other as other; ethics comes from love.

Love comes from mourning the loss of the love object.

It is not about self-sacrifice, pure devotion, or kindness for the sake of kindness; it is about becoming a loving subject.

***

Once, my enormously successful heart surgeon patient, who had just become a mother and who had lost her own mother at a very young age, elaborated beautifully and poetically on the longing for her own mother upon becoming a mother herself. This was definitely a Blues session: the heart surgeon managed to get to my heart.

Comedy is tragedy plus time. Give almost any tragedy time, and it has the potential to become a comedy. More than anything, the other side of the Blues is "jokes."

In melancholia you do not believe "this too shall pass," and hence you become a prisoner of time, of time that does not pass, of time that is left forever at 2:22: it does not tick, it does not move. In a sense it is like Groundhog Day: repetitive, boring, concrete, timeless, and without the possibility of a beyond which is not even sad, it is angry: not even a proper shade of Blue; maybe even red. So a mental conceptualization of time is the resolution of the Oedipus complex which ascertains the possibility of change. But this has also been the false promise of capitalism, so we have to be careful: if time does not get us in one way, it will try in another.

Notes

1 Forten, *Free Woman of Colour, Selections from 1854 to 1859*.
2 Bollas, *Cracking Up: Work of Unconscious Experience*.
3 Lemma, *Humour on the Couch: Exploring Humour in Psychotherapy and in Everyday Life*.
4 Freud, *Jokes and Their Relation to the Unconscious*.
5 Volkan, "From Earthquakes to Ethnic Cleansing: Societal Responses to Massive Traumas," in *Trauma, Trust, and Memory: Social Trauma and Reconciliation in Psychoanalysis, Psychotherapy and Cultural Memory*.
6 Freud, *Jokes and Their Relation to the Unconscious*.

Elle

Elle is my supervisee's patient. She was one hundred percent sure: because she was psychotic she did not know doubt, nor metaphor. She just knew, with conviction, that her analyst was the one writing love letters to her outside of the sessions on various social media apps in the format of a secret admirer. She was sure, and told him time after time that she understood and had compassion for his slip of ethics… he should just tell her, and they could get married.

I, the supervisor, the master in joining the unconscious of the patient, having been trained with the best modern psychoanalysts to a point that once my paranoid schizophrenic patient told me: "Dr. Homayounpour, you are really paranoid, you know that?" I found myself checkmated by the big, black, convinced eyes of Elle. When the analyst asked her: "What do these letters say?" Elle would respond: "Stop playing these games, you know what you write to me."

Our supervisory dyad became more and more desperate, so against my better judgment we even tried the cruelest of all methods. We attempted to introduce the reality principle to a psychotic structure, having to face once again the uselessness of such a method.

One day my supervisee told me: "Dr. Homayounpour, she is so convinced that sometimes I doubt myself, what if I am writing to her?" It got to the point where Elle said she would sue the analyst for unethical behavior unless he came clean and told her he loved her, just as in the content of his letters, so that they could get married and put this saga behind them. At this point I thought, and told my supervisee: well, it seems that our only solution is that you marry this beautiful girl; you are looking for a wife, aren't you?

But we thought of a more uncreative and professional response for our Elle. He told the heartbroken Elle, "It's not me who is writing to you. You're certainly allowed to think that if you wish, but I really enjoy our work together, and would like to continue working together." She replied: "Fine, if that's how you'd like to do it, it seems as if you have very perverse courting fantasies: let's pretend I'm your patient and you're my analyst…" Elle, oh Elle, how much I adored her and enjoyed hearing about her; she seemed to be

DOI: 10.4324/9781003269113-20

the only one of the three of us who could find a reasonable solution, so I said yes, tell her that is a wonderful idea, let's pretend, and pretend they did and this analytic couple did great work together.

After many months of pretending that he was the analyst and she the patient, one day my supervisee came to me and said: "I have great news: Elle came to her session today saying her neighbor's son has come forward and admitted to being her secret admirer." My supervisee and I were delighted; this was a good sign in every aspect of the treatment... the next session Elle walked in and told my supervisee that she had found out that it was the analyst who had hired the neighbor's boy to tell her these lies. She continued to say to my supervisee: "Oh my goodness, you really have time and money on your hands for such dramatic and twisted plots. If you continue with your bizarre ways, there will be no money left for our wedding."

Superego

If I met my superego at a party, I would not want to have anything to do with this boring, concrete, repetitive character. I would certainly excuse myself or signal to a friend to rescue me, but I have a hunch that this character in very outdated clothing, this character who is both feminine and masculine, would not be so easily eliminated. I could see this character cornering me and never shutting up. This redundant, tireless, and rude character, this annoying odd-ball of a personality intimately intertwined with melancholia.

DOI: 10.4324/9781003269113-21

Clean Your Eyeglasses

After all the efforts, the immense efforts that this stunning young girl had put into dressing up and putting full make-up on for him, jewelry and perfume and the whole nine yards, she walks in and sits down at the dinner table, attempting to move in the most seductive way she knows how. The moment she sits down, he says:

> You have to clean your eyeglasses. Look, I have these excellent pre-packaged cleaning devices, they are fantastic, you can buy them at any pharmacy, easy to use, practical, you can carry them everywhere with you, they fit right in your pocket.

DOI: 10.4324/9781003269113-22

Grandfather Blues

An intriguing story about the history of psychoanalysis in Iran began for me when I found out that there was a psychiatrist named Dr. Ali Falaati. He studied medicine in Geneva between the years 1914 and 1922, and traveled to Vienna at some point during this period, in the hope of meeting with Sigmund Freud. I could not find any information on whether that meeting ever took place, but upon his return to Iran, Dr. Falaati wrote a book entitled *From Hafez to Freud*.

My imagination runs wild. It was exactly during those years that my paternal grandfather was studying medicine in Geneva, and hence I can assume that he was friends with most of the Iranians at the medical school there, who were probably few in number. We can further imagine that they made their trip to visit Freud in 1917, the exact year of the publication of *Mourning and Melancholia*, and in an attempt to continue fantasizing about the alleged meeting, I presume that Dr. Falaati wouldn't have been able to refuse his best friend's request to join him at the greatly anticipated meeting at Berggasse 19, in Vienna's Ninth District. The two friends would have arrived at Freud's home and study, where he lived for over forty-seven years, in the building that is now probably Vienna's most famous address.

My grandfather was dealing with an unfinished mourning of his own, after the loss of his father at a very young age. There in Berggasse, did he hence secretly wish that the charismatic and by-then famous Professor Freud, author of the recently published *Mourning and Melancholia*, would work with him on his various shades of the Blues?

Just to think that there is that faint possibility that my grandfather's eyes, into which I remember staring on various occasions as a young child trying to figure him out, as he was such a mysterious figure… just to wonder if those very eyes had looked into Freud's eyes, had gazed upon him in Vienna. It is simply enchanting.

It reminds me of Roland Barthes, who elaborates, in a touching segment in *Camera Lucida*:

> One day, quite some time ago, I happened on a photograph of Napoleon's youngest brother, Jerome, taken in 1852. And I realized then, with

DOI: 10.4324/9781003269113-23

an amazement I have not been able to lessen since: "I am looking at eyes that looked at the Emperor." Sometimes I would mention this amazement, but since no one seemed to share it, nor even to understand it (life consists of these little touches of solitude), I forgot about it.[1]

Some might say that my sentiments with regard to Freud are quite fetishistic; this is the same accusation that was leveled upon me when I describe the uncanny feeling of entering Berggasse 19. Every single time, the same uncanniness is experienced. It never fails, not even after the multiple times that I have by now entered that space. To such charges, I must answer that they are a correct assessment of my sentiments: fetishistic they are.

Should we not be slightly fetishistic when it comes to our heritage? When considering our transgenerational lineage? Are these not the links that will navigate us beyond melancholia? I find that a sense of heritage is often what is fading from contemporary psychoanalysis. From the fear of being engulfed by the master, we find ourselves paradoxically drowning in melancholia.

How comical that when some folks talk about the history of psychoanalysis in Iran, they begin and end it with themselves: how lonely, how brief.

Note

1 Barthes, *Camera Lucida: Reflections on Photography.*

An Airport Taxi Driver in Tehran

A taxi driver in Tehran says: "They should stop the export of oil and start the import of tourists, this will rescue us."

The argument has been made that oil is the Iranian curse of the black diamond. I am not sure if he is right, but in any case, being right is overrated.

A patient internally contemplates, continuously, obsessively: "If only everybody believed me to be right about this…" She could never settle to the idea that she was wrong—not because she thought she was always right, but precisely because of the opposite reason. Deep down, she believed she was utterly wrong all of the time. Most of the time she was not even right about this assertion. She unconsciously thought she was completely wrong all the time, and so as a defense against falling apart, she had to pretend to herself and others, to make believe that she was right.

I felt very right about my assertions and my interpretations, and was surprised to find out how useless they were to her, all my correct interpretations. She only started to find me interesting when I gave up the pleasure of being right. The *morality* behind being right becomes a perverse moment, for at that moment you assign to yourself the position of the law. And that is the simple definition of perversion for Lacan: you become the law, you recognize the law of the other, but only to transgress it, not to subvert it (which would be absolutely magnificent, even coming close to a definition of freedom: to subvert, not to transgress). This is often a confused concept within modern art too: not only a problem of psychoanalysis, but perhaps even a symptom of our contemporaneity.

DOI: 10.4324/9781003269113-24

A Reliable, Silent Nanny

A colleague/friend was telling me about her nanny, who takes care of her twin boys while my friend goes to work. This is what she said:

> Help me, Gohar, she refuses to say more than a word here or there to me. I want her to approve of me, to think I am a worthy mother, to compliment me; isn't that bizarre? Shouldn't it be the other way around?
>
> In a very critical voice, she said to me the other day: "You don't put rose petals in your tea. Also, I notice that the boys' feet smell because I saw you once wipe their feet with a towel instead of washing them, when they came back from kindergarten. The only way the smell will go away now is if you put dry teabags in their shoes overnight."

I thought: whatever is going on between my friend and her nanny, the signifier of "tea" seems to be a crucial one for the nanny.

My friend continued:

> In the history of psychoanalysis, even the most orthodox, old-school analysts have never been as silent as my nanny is with me.
>
> This is how a typical conversation goes:

I:	How are you feeling today?
The nanny:	Well.
I:	Let me tell you what happened when I was driving today; driving in this city is insane, it makes me so mad... [trying to make conversation].
The nanny:	Oh.
I:	Do you feel like that sometimes while you drive?
The nanny:	Shall I make chicken or lamb for the boys tonight?

I want to ask her: "Do you love me?" To which, I would assume, she would respond in a neutral, robotic tone of voice, "Certainly, *Madame.*"

DOI: 10.4324/9781003269113-25

My friend goes on:

> Are you wondering why I care if the nanny loves me or not? Why do I
> tolerate this sadomasochistic relationship? Maybe you even think she
> reminds me of my critical mother?

I say I had not had such thoughts. I was, however, intrigued to hear more, as
nanny conversations intrigue me. It is never clear who is at the mercy of whom;
the nature of the relationship seems to me to be such a breeding ground for very
complicated layers of psychic dynamics to come to the fore. The relationship
with one's nanny is the ultimate Foucauldian liaison.

My desperate colleague goes on,

> Ohhh… My nanny is the nightmare of my life, for she is reliable, clean,
> and consistent. In four years she has never forgotten to put rose petals in
> my tea, she does not have a smartphone, is never late, and is completely
> attentive to my kids.

I say, well, isn't that a relief? If she doesn't have a phone that means if she's
not talking to you, at least she's not talking to anyone else either.

My friend, now with a touch of humor in her voice, says: "You know, when
I receive gifts, cards or flowers from people I leave them around for her to see,
so she can witness that I am loved by many."

She passionately continues:

> My nanny is always on time, never takes a sick day, the boys are fed on the
> dot every day, fruit and all… sometimes I hear her gently talking to them
> while they're all playing together. This does not happen often, but I think
> she speaks to my boys more than she speaks to her husband. The boys are
> very safe with her; she is not fun or stimulating, they don't run around and
> laugh together, but they count on her reliability; she is always there, in her
> black outfit, waiting for them, water and fruit in hand, the moment their
> kindergarten bell rings. She is eternally there, somber-looking, as faithful to
> her melancholia as she is to my boys.

In Praise of Hopelessness

After some years of analysis, Ms. E said to me in a session:

> You know, the hopelessness in analysis is not about the rule of "absen-tia," which is part and parcel of psychoanalysis. It's about the fact that time applies to analysts too, that you all get older, that a day will come when you and I will both die, that our bodies are failing us as we speak…

I, the analyst, say: So, you are saying that we have limitations…

I think of the stage she is at in her analysis, where a separation/individua-tion and hence an Oedipalization seems to be unfolding. I have a hunch that this new stage is precisely what has brought up hopelessness, the concept of time, and limitations into her associations.

She goes on:

> You sound better. (I had a cold during her sessions last week.) My mother is better too, she has started shopping again, so that's a clear sign that she has recovered from her heart issue. It was very helpful what you said in my last session about the timing of my mother's heart problems resurfacing exactly as I was graduating from my doctorate program; she was hospitalized the exact day of my graduation. I felt like we were moving somewhere and then we all regressed: you got sick, she got sick…

Ms. E continues:

> I had a very strange dream:
>
> In the dream, my father was still living with us in our childhood home, so he had not yet left us to live in France; our home was full of very French-looking furniture. One of my husband's friends, a very irrespon-sible man in reality, arrives on a horse to take us to the Bazaar in North Tehran, because we had to go there to get a piece of paper stamped, and that stamped document would give my father permission to stay in Iran. So we get there, and we were "parking" the horse, but because the horse

DOI: 10.4324/9781003269113-26

was parked where people were coming and going, the police took the horse away; it was illegal where we had parked.

I was feeling desperate, because the papers had been on the horse that was taken away. At that moment I woke up with anxiety, and at the moment of waking I was thinking in the dream: why did I let this irresponsible guy drive us for such an important endeavor? and why did I allow him to break the law?

She then continues, associating to a childhood memory of being six years old and riding a horse. It ended up in a horrible accident in which she was hit by another horse as she got off her own horse. It was a horrible blow that destroyed her knee. After that, although she is a fierce animal lover, she became phobic of horses.

Then suddenly Ms. E says:

You know, in the last few months I have finally been referred male patients, they come and remain in psychotherapy with me. I was not able to keep male patients before, even when I got a referral, but the referrals were mostly women too: this has also changed. I have actually begun to get a great deal of positive feedback from my male patients.

I, the analyst, say: it seems a part of you has gotten your papers stamped after all; has gotten permission to enjoy being with men.

Ms. E responds:

I don't know how, but I feel it has something to do with Oedipus, the triangulation we have been talking about... I feel you are on the side of Oedipus... I feel like you are ok with me having relationships with men, I feel allowed, as if you have given me permission...

I, the analyst, highlight: *Permission... Police.*

She goes on: "I forgot to tell you this part of the dream: I also cooked for my father in our old home; you can't imagine how pleasurable it felt to cook for him."

I reflect to myself, since she omitted this last part in the first telling of the dream: How allowed does she really feel by me to cook for her father, to be an Oedipal girl? However, she is able to remember it now. There definitely is a conflict, but in her dream her father does not get his permission papers signed to be allowed to stay, and it is her dream after all. How conflictual it is for her to have him stay and to cook for him, or for him to leave, as he did in reality, leaving her, her sisters and mother in an enmeshed negative Oedipus of their own: one in which she would ambivalently become the husband of a very fragile, incapable mother with various and continuing health problems, and a mother/father to her two younger sisters.

Is she struggling with the emergence of the possibility of having permission to be Oedipal, in a classic sense, finally? It is something which a part of her deeply desires and another part fiercely rejects, and fears.

I, the analyst, say: You don't think at some level you were already Oedipal by the time your father left?

> Yes, the pleasure of cooking for my dad in the dream was familiar, but scary.

I continue: Something leads to the loss of permission in your dream; there seems to be a forbiddingness regarding these pleasures, having permission for such pleasures, so another part of you takes that permission away.
Ms. E:

> This reminds me: the permission was about how long my father could stay in our home, not in Iran, as I said at first... My husband's friend is a lazy guy, and he was trying to ride down the wrong side of the road; he reminded me, in the dream, of my mother.
> (I, the analyst, think of the other side of the road as reverse Oedipus; lazy is always associated for her with her overweight and sick mother.)

The question seems to be: does she have permission to go back/ahead to see what would have happened to her Oedipus if her father had stayed at home? She seems to be contemplating laws, transgressions, what is prohibited, what is permitted; what are the punishments of such forbidden pleasures, of wanting your father to stay, of wanting to cook for him? All these are questions which emerge upon entering the Oedipal scene. The horse is a symbol of the unconscious and its forbidden wishes, but the horse breaks her knee. She is punished for her prohibited wishes, within the metaphor of the phobia of horses deeply rooted in our psychoanalytic heritage within the case of "Little Hans," the little boy who became phobic of horses due to fears of castration, castration performed in his mind by his father as a punishment for his forbidden Oedipal wishes.[1] At this particular moment in time, in a psychoanalyst's office in Tehran, our subject, Ms. E, is scared of her mother's potential vengeful fury.

I wonder with her what would have happened if the dream had continued? It was so pleasurable at the beginning; what if the pleasure had been sustained? What if the permission had not gotten lost...? To which she responds: "If the permission had not been lost, my mother would have been lost, and that makes my heart fall..."

Your heart, I highlight, making an allusion to the mother's heart problems... Ms. E says: "I can't even fantasize any further, even fantasizing about it gets daunting..."

Ms. E continues: "I wish we did not have to end today's session; I wish it could go on forever…"

I think to myself: This could be a regressive wish to go back to the fusional paradise with the mother, to the pre-Oedipal stage of her analysis with me, where fathers do not get permission to stay, and there is no concept of time or limits yet. It could also be her way of trying to tell me she still wants to be with me, that she still needs me. She could be saying: don't worry, I will stay with you forever.

She is always complaining about her mother not letting her go, wanting to spend time with her, even now that she is married, asking her to live close by and to visit her every day and take care of all her errands. Whatever the reality of her mother, in the dream it becomes clear that these laments of hers have a projective function. It is Ms. E who is conflicted between her desire to be her mother's mother, husband, and lover and the new/old possibilities of triangulation that are emerging via her analysis that allow her to re-find old pleasures once experienced and then forgotten, and now remembered.

In the middle of these thoughts, I had an association to the early years of her analysis, when she would keep bringing various fresh fruit juices to her sessions for me. After a couple of years, one day she brought me fruits instead of fruit juice. That's when I told her: Wow! We have progressed; it seems that you have the idea that now I can finally tolerate solid food.

Ms. E ends her session that day: "Today's session had the affect of my dream: pleasurable and yet it has to stop."

She started and finished her session with limitations: this is where she is at… *limitations*, which lead to the beginning of difference via renunciation.

The violent moment of separation brings with it possibilities of integration, but immense sadness as well. It is a gateway to mourning, which is why Melanie Klein called it the "Depressive Position."[2] In order for us to be able to mourn the loss of the loved object, we have to have come face-to-face with absence, frustrations, sadness, and, above all, renunciation. We have to renounce the fusional, Utopian world of primary narcissism in order to access various shades of the "Blues." In short, I would define Lacan's *jouissance*, which is in the territory of the death drive, as the wish for a lack of renunciation.[3]

Freedom is not about limitless possibilities, it is about choice, about choosing. Freedom is not about transgressing prohibitions imposed on our pleasure, but submitting to these prohibitions, otherwise we are thrown into the pit of "surplus-enjoyment," to continue with Lacan, which brings with it nothing but eroticized pain.[4]

As such, hope becomes very problematic. The symptomatology of hope is a continent not too far away from *jouissance*. Essentially, if one looks at the Freudian map of the psyche, they share clear borders. For you can hope for your immortality, hope for an Oedipal triumph, hope for limitless possibilities of enjoyment, of limitless choices, hope for a re-finding of a fusional relationship with our primary love object, hope for a life without frustration, without separation, hope for limitless possibilities within yourself and the other. In short, we can say that hope is intertwined with *jouissance* and excess pleasure, in the territory of death, while hopelessness has a clear link to renunciation, choice, pleasure, and life. Thus Nietzsche says: "Hope in reality is the worst of all evils because it prolongs the torments of man."[5] But this Nietzschean cornerstone should not be read as a pessimistic nor a nihilistic position; on the contrary, it is a *yes* to life, an affirmation of an active pessimist, a passionate pessimist, for life awaits only the hopeless; hope becomes a defense to living a passionate life.

This is not existential pessimism, it is realism, and we know by now what happens to those who do not reach the reality principle: they will not get their passport stamped on the gates to the pleasure principle, and they will be destined for / detained within the land of the imaginary, of paranoia and delusions.

Once I was telling L about my love for airports as transitional spaces where everything seems possible, for every arrival at a destination becomes an imposition on my freedom to be elsewhere. It is only in transitional spaces that you have the possibility of arriving anywhere. My wise friend said: "But that is like an adolescent fantasy indicating you want to be *everywhere*; such a fantasy indicates: I do not want obstacles imposed on my freedom," and she was right. I thought that these fantasies were some sort of defense against the anxiety that accompanies the dizziness of freedom. There is nothing scarier than getting close to one's desire. For as Lacan has taught us, anxiety is the only real affect, the affect that does not lie.

Perhaps for Ms. E it is not just about Oedipus *per se*, perhaps it is more of a narcissistic projection: "My mother's heart will stop working if I separate from her." Another elaboration could go something like this: My heart cannot take losing my current position with regard to her. Perhaps it is the guilt of existence, of having desires of her own, of experiencing pleasure in general, the guilt of having subjectivity, the guilt of having the wish to separate (we already acknowledged the fear of separation dormant within her). It could go something like this: if you find out that I want to be separate, you will be vengeful, you will punish me. I am a bad girl, for I have wanted to kill my mother: this is how Julia Kristeva elaborates on matricide. She discusses how, as a defense against this necessary act of matricide on our way to subjectivity, we end up living where they live, in order not to respond to or to deny this primary desire to leave. As I said above, this elaboration very much encompasses the essence of melancholia.

The guilt of separateness, the guilt of existence, the guilt of subjectivity. Hence Ms. E saying: "If I did not lose permission," (in this new elaboration we could say: if I did not lose permission to exist) "then my mother would get lost."

There is a qualitative difference to this guilt, although it could certainly also be seen as a defense against Oedipalization.

A few sessions after the session above, Ms. E had a dream that she was voraciously eating a mango, associating this to a story by Sudhir Kakar on a myth about one of the most popular Hindu gods, Ganesha:

> A mango was floating down the stream and Uma, the mother, said that whoever rode around the universe first would receive the mango. Skanda impulsively gets on his golden peacock and goes around the universe, but Ganesha contemplates his mother's motivation, then circumnutates her, announcing: "I have gone around my universe."[6]

Ms. E goes on: "Clearly Ganesha was our winner of the mango."

Again, besides the many layers of interpretation, it is important to hear what Ms. E is remembering from the myth and what she is "forgetting." For example, she omits here that in the myth, upon his first bite of the mango, Ganesha breaks his tusks.

For me, the mango dream beautifully encapsulates her questions around subjectivity: What is she allowed? What is prohibited? And, ultimately, what is the universe made of? Is a man allowed to stay? Does he get his papers stamped to stay or does he have to go (man-go)?

It seems that Ms. E has already added Sudhir Kakar, India, erotic fruits, and the mesmerizing, magical Indian mythology to our analytic room. That is delicious already: what a momentous and welcomed arrival, floating down the stream from lands far, far away.

Notes

1 Freud, *Complete Psychological Works of Sigmund Freud.*
2 Klein, "A Contribution to the Psychogenesis of Manic-Depressive States."
3 Lacan and Fink, *Écrits: The First Complete Edition in English.*
4 Lacan and Grigg, *The Seminar of Jacques Lacan: The Other Side of Psychoanalysis.*
5 Nietzsche, *Human, All Too Human.*
6 Kakar, *Indian Identity.*

Blues Shuffle / Swing *or* Off-Beats

The Blues shuffle is made up of eighth notes alternating between a long and a short note. The long note falls on the beat. The shorter note is in between, and comes in on the upbeat. You are playing an eighth-note triplet but leaving out the middle note. Simply that.

What greatly consoles the parts of me that feel I have made a great many mistakes with you as a mother, that (gratefully for both of us) I have been far from ideal, and to think you will be given the freedom to be proudly, freely, pleasurably permitted to be flawed when you become a mother yourself one day. (Yes, I have that desire for you, yes, I have dreamed it.) Then perhaps your children, in turn, will become not only great swimmers of the wild seas but also competent deep divers, and this is how we attempt to break out of the tunnel of horror of perfections, goodness, and idealizations, with the word "tunnel" purposefully chosen here. Perhaps our grandchildren will become sailors.

The other day you told me, in quite a serious voice: "Mommy, please go to work, you are too much when you are home a lot." How we laughed together, for I knew you were right.

Then sometimes when I am at work you miss me, and you get jealous of all these people that you have to share my libido with, and you ask that I take you to work. What is it really that Mommy does, behind this closed door? What is this exciting profession that becomes a seamless scenario of the primal scene? and you want to hear and see what is going on... probably mostly to hear, a signifier of the spirit of psychoanalysis.

Let us "shuffle" now: what happens to patients via the analyst's pregnancy? Well, to some, absolutely nothing, so let us say that first.

If we look at the main psychoanalytic literature on the analyst's pregnancy—which I never personally liked, as I found it frequently to be too narcissistic on the analyst's part—it is mostly in the realm of the patients' envy, pre-Oedipal dynamics, regressions, wanting to be inside your belly, wanting to kill your baby, and feverish at you for having a life of your own, desires outside of them, and—God forbid—being sexual. All of which is certainly true, as always, depending on the unconscious fantasy of the analysand, and where they find themselves in their analysis.

DOI: 10.4324/9781003269113-27

However: something that I was not able to find anything written on, and that I personally experienced during my pregnancies with patients, is, in short, a sense of *relief* at the sight of the analyst's pregnancy. Many patients associated feeling delighted at this new site of vitality, life, and libido. For some, this confirmed the presence of a strong parental couple, a couple who desire each other and therefore will allow the children to run wild with all kinds of fantasies. There is nothing as reassuring as the presence of a desirous parental couple for families, no matter what the family constellation might look like.

My pregnancies, it seemed to me, gave a new sense of freedom for many patients to become Oedipal in the transference; the relief of the encounter of the third in our relationship permitted them to challenge this very third. The third came into the room via the pregnancy of the analyst, and not only were they not wholly angry that their analyst had desires outside of them, they welcomed it with open arms, only later to challenge it, fight with it, fantasize about the qualities of this very third, and eventually, God willing, to identify with a third.

A male patient started telling me about his erotic transference:

> Now that you are pregnant, you feel less dangerous; you and I are not alone in this room, for not only is the baby present, but it is present because someone you desire enough to have a child with has impregnated you.

This man had a serious conflict around incest: *too close* would always become colored with incestuous desires, and the moment we discussed termination he felt as if he was going to literally die. My pregnancy opened up a third choice for him (again, we know that the analyst's pregnancy can become such a gateway only because of the many years of previous work and where the analysand is at that point in the analysis; hence my first pregnancy did not have such an effect on this patient—timing is indeed everything). He was the last of five children, he had never seen his mother pregnant, he was certain she never had sex with his father after he was born, as she was too busy putting him to her breast and fondling his penis. They slept in the same bed for many years, and he was breast-fed until he was seven years old, teeth and all. One day when my pregnant stomach was too big for him to ignore (although some other patients did manage to do exactly that throughout the pregnancy), after a few months of deep melancholia, he was also able to discuss the relief that came with the sight of my pregnancy. He said:

> How lucky are people who get to see their mother pregnant, what a relief, what a delight! Now I can finally fight with my dead father, who has become invigorated, enlivened via your pregnancy. Now I can tell you all my fantasies, knowing that this third being between us, whoever he/she is, will protect me, will protect you, will protect us.

Another patient, who was harboring various fantasies about my getting a divorce, as he was certain I was sleeping in my office, said, upon my pregnancy: "I was wishing for your divorce, and that very wish made me extremely anxious." He was having episodes of panic attacks, terrified that I might be getting a divorce and that he might re-experience an ill-fated, doomed Oedipal triumph, leaving him no choice but to blind himself.

Another analysand said: "You are sexual, oh my God, I have always respected you, but sexual you were not." It became a gateway for him to work on a very classic split of the Madonna–whore complex, where he has begun to integrate sexuality with love and respect.

I found that many patients were not envious but relieved, for they had passed this stage in their lives: "The burps, the night feeds, what a long road you have ahead of you," one patient said to me.

A female patient, in the midst of a very negative transference upon my pregnancy, playfully said: "You are erotic after all, not just meticulously studious, what a relief, let's start having fun!" The sessions which followed clearly became libidinized.

Surely there are so many levels of interpretation to what these patients are saying, and surely one should never take at face value what the patient is saying. We have to attempt to hear all that is being said between the lines, the negations, the repression, and... ultimately, the unconscious fantasy, and yet I think it is noteworthy to think about the analyst's pregnancy, at times, also as the arrival of a third into the room, taking the atmosphere of the room far from the very oft-discussed pre-Oedipal issues associated with analysts' pregnancies, or with pregnancies in general for that matter.

The arrival of this third will be the beginning of mourning, will allow the building blocks of our boats (and even ships) to be foreshadowed. It will form the possibilities of "linkings," of lineage, of heritage, of sails to be set. Aristotle wrote in *The Politics*:

> A ship which is only a span long will not be a ship at all, nor a ship a quarter of a mile long; yet there may be a ship of a certain size, either too large or too small, which will still be a ship, but bad for sailing.[1]

According to Freud, a little child becomes a scientist the moment that they first *want to know*: the moment they become curious about how babies are made. We become interested in knowledge because of secrets; without secrets we are sentenced to a transplant dyad "beyond the pleasure principle." In today's socio-political climate, we are pigeonholed into a dyadic, claustrophobic relationship where mothers never leave, fathers do not intervene, and where our parents' bedroom doors are open because they have decided to be cool and liberal, even if that means destroying all that the child might experience about curiosity, intimacy, discovery, creativity, and, above all, the possibility of fantasizing about the primal scene.

I always find it tragic when I hear analysts ask their patients to tell them everything. *EVERYTHING*—not that such a thing would be possible, but to make such a demand on anyone—on your patient, your child, your lover— terrifies me.

This calls to mind Foucault's Panopticon.[2] Prisoners inside the Panopticon are seen without the ability to see. Not unlike the analytic couch, it was used as an effective method of torture, because to be under surveillance at all times is the real death of the subject. There is a clear dynamic of power that has shifted, and it raises the question of what can then be presumed about the analytic couch. Remember: Freud said that after all is said and done, one needs to have at least a little masochism to lie on the analytic couch.

I was pleased to find out that the color Persian Indigo, which was also called regimental, was called by that name because it used to be the color of the *naval* uniforms of several nations in the late nineteenth and early twen- tieth centuries. If one has to choose to be a soldier, it is best to be in the navy, in the impassioned sea, dressed in a Persian Indigo uniform, where recogniz- ing the uncanny unconscious is *unheimlich*: in final analysis not only myster- ious, but also strangely familiar. Locating the strangeness in the ordinary, locating the mystery, the strangeness, at home, in the domesticated, across the tamed, upon the un-belonging, and resulting in an irreducible anxiety.

Once a colleague asked me: "Do you think it is appropriate that you write about your life? What will your patients think?"

I was surprised that her ordinary mysteriousness as an analyst was so fra- gile to her, and, she assumed, to her patients. I thought of a supervisee who called in for her supervision one day distressed that she had encountered her patient at the beach, and, to make matters worse, wearing a bikini. Oh my, how troubling after all... the analysis was over; what was she going to do now? All naked, all stripped of her *Unheimlichkeit*.

I wanted to tell my colleague: first of all, I could be making it all up as I write. Second, do we not believe that it does not matter what one says or does outside the session, but only what you say or do inside the session, as that is the communication to our analysands? I have always thought that even if our diaries were to be found and read by our patients, it would not matter at all. They would read their own book into the diary, they would do their own shuffle or swing, fitting us in perfectly as the very substitutable objects of their phantasm.

This does not mean that the reality of the analyst does not matter; it cer- tainly does. We are flawed mortals, but this reality is not nearly as significant, nor as central, as many contemporary psychoanalysts would like us to believe. In general, *we are not that central* is a basic and fundamental Freudian message.

At times, these days, the reality of the psychoanalyst becomes pivotal to the point where we are coming to have only one person in the analytic room, and that is our lonely analyst.

If we choose to write about our patients, it cannot be from an arrogant point of view. It has to be hospitable, we have to have the courage to write about ourselves—with any luck, not as the center of it all, but as a dislocated, stateless Caliban in the margin, where our uncanniness is not a fragile piece of porcelain but an inherent part of what we do as psychoanalysts.

The same colleague who morally objected to my writing of "private matters" absolutely believes in self-disclosures on the part of the analyst inside the analytic room as an often used and valuable technique.

Besides, I like to write about real/ordinary life. I find nothing to be as enthralling, adhering, desirous of a magical realness: not the exoticized kind, but the one favored by the unconscious.

Gabriel García Márquez beautifully elaborates on such a necessity:

> It always amuses me that the biggest praise for my work comes for the imagination, while the truth is that there's not a single line in all my work that does not have a basis in reality. The problem is that Caribbean reality resembles the wildest imagination.[3]

I am certain that the same thing could be said about the uncanny unconscious of my geography, and that of yours, of every single one of us, resembling the wildest of imaginations.

Playing *with swing*, or *with a shuffle feel*, means to play with swung eighths (or to employ "triplet feel" eighths) which means that the first eighth of a beat gets a longer duration than the second. Also, off-beats are generally emphasized, or syncopated.

Medium Persian Blue, a kind of dark blue which is referred to as Persian Indigo, Dark Persian Blue or Regimental.

How much pleasure is she allowed to have before it becomes unsafe for her and the ones she loves, she melancholically hesitates... or does she feel that she is getting away with something, so she undoes the happiness in order to regain control?

I imagine her: she was nine years old, standing behind the window ornate with dark Persian Blue curtains, looking down on the street from her grandparents' third-floor apartment. It was rush hour, and the street was filled with cars going back and forth at a very high speed; she was desperately trying to search for the silhouette of her mother, that walk... that pace... desperately trying to locate the familiar sound of her heels... but from where she was standing, that was plainly impossible: the sidewalk was so far away, the noises were too inhospitable to our young girl's beating heart, as she waited for her mother to arrive home. To arrive from where? That is the question.

Our nine-year-old heroine never gave up, no matter how crowded the street, how flamboyant the noises. In the midst of this impossibility, with palpitating anxiety, she would time after time suddenly trust that she had located her mother, only to find herself betrayed by her naïve faith. For as the image got closer, the woman would become a stranger, simply a stranger, not her mother after all. Again and again this sequence would repeat itself, until suddenly her mother would appear, there in flesh, to play hide-and-seek with her in between the dark Persian Blue curtains. To my imagined girl's surprise, she would think to herself: How did I miss you? I kept looking for you, I did not even hear or notice when you came in… How is it possible that I missed you? You, whom I was searching for with every cell of my being. Suddenly all the background music of the house was enlivened with the mother's arrival and the sound of her heels… even the curtains looked happier, having turned a more jolly, less ambivalent shade of blue.

This is a girl who has trouble going to school; she holds on to her mother and cries for hours, and the only way she is willing to attend her classes is if the mother remains in the school garden. She sometimes goes to the window of her classrooms to make sure her mother is still there, and her mother always is.

Mothers who abandon their kids are never mothers who have a life of their own; often they are precisely the mothers who are too fusional, too controlling, too overinvested, and many other toos (twos). And so they leave: they abandon their kids in a genuine attempt for—a shot at—thirdness. Unfortunately, often things don't end up working out that way, but there is a genuine unconscious attempt at a cure which lies hidden within the often ignored or simplified moralistic discourse of mothers who abandon their kids. This does not mean one should not consider the various socio-politico-historical levels of such a discourse, either. It is, however, striking to think that mothers could abandon their kids, wishing to free themselves and their kids from such a claustrophobic dyad. From this outlook, could we also entertain the possibility that alive in an abandonment fantasy, whether it is acted upon or not, there is a clear wish for all parties involved to breathe? To take a breath.

Notes

1 Aristotle, *The Politics*, 1326.
2 Foucault, *Discipline and Punish: The Birth of the Prison*.
3 García Márquez, interviewed by Stone, "The Art of Fiction No. 69."

Galway Girl

He told me the other day that he loves her, oh, how he loves those blue eyes and long black hair. He has seen her only twice in his life, and about a decade ago. These are the things he remembers most from those two encounters:

The first time they had dinner at a small restaurant; all he remembers is that she was wearing white pants with a striped shirt *à la marinière*, he tells me:

> You know, a little South-of-France-y, which was a bit strange for a meeting in Ireland. She had the most incredible smell, a combination of coconut and vanilla, reminiscent of summer days by the sea. She looked stunning, but with these high heels, totally inappropriate for the occasion.

She was intelligent, dialogical, challenging, precise. Full of grace and laughter, but also directness and challenge. He watched her femininity diligently, and the almost imperceptible movement of her shoulders when she took a breath. He remembers watching her intensely, memorizing her, terrified that the night would end and he wouldn't be able to see her ever again.

The second time they met, at an Irish pub, he was fifty minutes late (a whole Freudian hour), for at the moment he was leaving his hotel room to meet her, he had a very bizarre accident which led to his foot bleeding quite heavily. She was so young then: twenty-seven years old, to be exact. He remembers with precision the way she moved her body, her hands with those slender fingers. How anxious she would become, trying to impress him intellectually, and she said brilliant deep philosophical things that did not match her age, with a certainty that is part and parcel of youth.

I ask him if it was love at first sight, then? "No," he replies, annoyed at my question: he always finds me a bit of a pain when it comes to talking about her, too much on the side of fantasy as opposed to action... so he says:

> No, it was not love at first sight at all, I have no idea how it happened. It was love before first sight. All I know is that I am certain that there is no other like her, she is my destiny, and is this not the only simple definition

DOI: 10.4324/9781003269113-28

of love? When you have the conviction, no matter how illusory, that there is not another person who even remotely resembles the beloved? It is the first time in my life that I am not in a power relation, I want nothing, and I want to give her everything, whatever she desires, no questions asked. (I think: how unfortunate for my friend, I worry for him.)

They *just* write to each other, often extraordinary letters; he can't stop going over the email she wrote to him yesterday; he can't stop thinking about her; he needs to feel her close… He does not want to be fixated in a melancholic longing, he wants to touch her—not just once, that is just in stories. He wants ordinary things with her: he wants to have breakfast with her, he wants to read to her, he wants to wake up next to her, he wants to prepare her a cup of coffee. She is so particular about her coffee, he is sure. Such an agony she can be. She probably takes too long to get ready; he longs to watch her get ready, he needs to inhale her. She is not too hot, nor too cold, just the precise desired warm temperature. He wants to go swimming with her, for my friend is an exceptional swimmer.

This is what her email of yesterday said, the one that has unsettled my friend:

> My Darling,
> Will we ever see each other again? Please know, please believe me that you eroticize me, for the last decade, we were supposed to meet three more times, twice you canceled at the last minute and once I canceled after I had booked my ticket to Galway, and every time, from the thought of being with you and being touched by you, I got pregnant.
> You do not belong to me, you belong to no one, you are an amphibious poet, belonging only to Ireland and Yeats, to Beckett and Joyce. But you eroticize me, mind and body, I do not need you to say "no" for me anymore, I do not need you to stand guard over my solitude, you must radically claim me.

As my enamored friend is talking, I have an association to a joyful fall afternoon when the Freudian Group of Tehran was gathered together in Mashhad; for Salman Akhtar, the prominent psychoanalyst, was visiting us from Philadelphia to generously give our candidates hours and hours of psychoanalytic seminars. I think of that afternoon in Mashhad now, for at one point he was talking about eroticism in the analytic room, and he said:

> It's not erotic for me if a female patient is overtly, concretely talking about sexual matters, but a patient the other day said to me: "Professor Akhtar, I would like to come by Sunday afternoon, and together we can organize your library."

He said: "Now that I found erotic."

I tell my friend: you know if a woman tells a man: just the thought of you touching me made me pregnant, that is splendidly erotic. But I cannot stop myself adding mischievously: reading that line, you probably did not envision what would have happened to your life of Beckett, Joyce, and swimming if her three kids had actually been yours. My friend is wicked enough to laugh with me at my mischievousness.

Who knows, I might just be experiencing a touch of jealousy.

I say: What was your response to her last erotic email?

"I just wrote her back: 'What can I hold you with? I offer you...' from 'Two English Poems' by Jorge Luis Borges.

I just wrote the below lines to her:

What do I have to offer you, to make you mine? Me, a disillusioned man conversing with the lonely moon; staring at it and holding on to it as if my life depends on it. I can offer you my forefathers, my fierce ancestors, my ghosts, I hold you like a wish.

I could offer you, my father's father and his mother's grandfather, both killed in battles in Buenos Aires, or in Peru (what difference does it make?), with bullets in their lung, or shot while leading a legion of hundreds of men. I could offer you the secrets of my books, the pain of my poems. I could offer you the faithfulness of a man who has never been faithful, the softest part of myself, the essence, the core, the part which I have somehow saved until now, for you. I can offer you the recollection of a rose that bloomed long before you were born. I can look into your soul, read you, tell you things you ignore and refuse to know about yourself and give you the loneliness that makes us so dark and our hearts so hungry. Allow me to seduce you with uncertainty, with precariousness and defeat. As I insist on holding you like a wish.[1]

I was struck by my friend's use of "just": he *just* offered her everything, mostly things he did not have: a more apt definition of love.

Salman Akhtar told us a great deal of wonderful stories on his Iranian voyage; he even sang us many poems in Urdu. I have been privileged enough to travel with our numerous visitors over the years, hearing countless incredible stories—the best ones were always told on the plane or during our taxi rides; to see their reactions to Iran, to hear their conversations with our students: so many memories, so many stories. So many friends and colleagues came to visit us, too many to name here. But their hospitable desire to be with us, to be together in good times and in bad times, oh, the laughs, the dinners, the encounters, the Isfahan Blues, will be forever part of the inheritance of psychoanalysis in Iran.

On our plane journey together from Mashhad to Tehran, Akhtar told me an astonishing story of how he had met Masoud Khan, an absolutely brilliant and dislocated Pakistani-British psychoanalyst, who had troubles of the soul and broke the psychoanalytic frame time after time. Neither the British Psychoanalytic Society nor the International Psychoanalytic Association has been hospitable or generous to him. For how can we not be hospitable to the genius part of a man because he has committed ethical violations? This is the paradox of the humanism of our times. I find it brutally moral, quite unethical. Our contemporary humanism is missing *irony*.

Note

1   Borges, *Selected Poems.*

Borges' Animals and Cemeteries

Borges describes a certain Chinese Encyclopedia, "the Celestial Emporium of Benevolent Knowledge."

What awaits us all is a tiny place in a cemetery...

In the cemeteries where Borges notices that each and every being, emperors or pharaohs,

Baby pigs or beautiful mermaids,

Legendary beings or poor stray dogs,

When alive, from afar, they all looked like insignificant flies

Later on, they will all fall, into the dark abyss

Right after a so-called "insignificant" but highly symbolic incident:

Breaking a flower vase.[2]

Borges' list shatters all familiarity, it becomes "an-other" space, and reminds me of Michel Foucault's elaborations on cemeteries in "Of Other Spaces" (airports, favorite spaces of mine, are also *other* spaces) in which he says that until we believed in immortality, the resurrection of bodies and the existence of a soul, what happened to our body's remains was insignificant.[3] From the moment that we are no longer sure of any of the above assertions, the dead body becomes sacred; hence it is since the beginning of the nineteenth century that everyone has gained a right to her or his own little box for her or his own little personal decay. Yet, from that very same moment, a clear obsession with death as an illness has developed. Foucault goes on to say:

> The dead, it is supposed, bring illnesses to the living, and it is the presence and proximity of the dead right beside the houses, next to the church, almost in the middle of the street, it is this proximity that propagates death itself. This major theme of illness spread by the contagion in the cemeteries persisted until the end of the eighteenth century, until, during the nineteenth century, the shift of cemeteries toward the suburbs was initiated. The cemeteries then came to constitute, no longer the sacred and immortal heart of the city, but the other city, where each family possesses its dark resting place.

DOI: 10.4324/9781003269113-29

Notes

1 Borges, *Collected Fictions.*
2 Borges, *Collected Fictions.*
3 Foucault, "Of Other Spaces: Utopias and Heterotopias."

Beyond Persian Blues...

Then I dreamt of *Anahita*...

I imagine this scene: my father, Duke Ellington, and Milan Kundera's father, Ludvik Kundera, are sitting in a Persian Garden in Isfahan. Duke Ellington is humming his lyrics to "Isfahan Blues":

The lights of dusk and twilight, with their purple hue, touching your heart and reminding you of the distance between you and your beloved, as the little stars ascend the sky.

The beloved, wandering in faraway places but leaving an immortal song; immortal, yet belonging to sparkling yesterdays, stardust of a love.

Then come the lonely nights, when, for new inspirations and for singing new songs, all one can do is float back in reveries to that muse that once was, with those inspirational kisses that no longer exist, the stardust of a song.

Isfahan, an earthly paradise, with its famed gardens, its celebrated nightingales and even more memorable roses, sings the song of a paradise lost, that maybe never was;

Stardust of a love song.

Ludvik seems frustrated by this choice of music, by this entire Blues project, and he switches the background music to none other than Leoš Janáček, and they all say together: "It's strange, it's strange," for Milan Kundera's father had trouble finding words for things at the end of his life: at the very end he lost nearly all his vocabulary. He could only say: "That's strange."

Father, I have built a boat and crossed beyond, and there are moments when I will allow myself to regress like a crazy person in an airport (an-other space), searching for you, breathlessly following a man who walks like you, and has a hat just like yours, and your khaki jacket, for quite some time before he turns around, slapping me in the face with the reality principle.

I am at my bluest when you do not get to see Darya laugh, when you do not see her running after butterflies, as you and I did together... when I don't get to tell you her funny Oedipal stories. But I tell her stories about you all

DOI: 10.4324/9781003269113-30

the time... how you taught me about shadows and light, and how you had the conviction that reading some books was more important than the bread on one's table (even though this does not seem to register with her yet).

Someday, I will tell her that you told me financial independence is what women's emancipation is about.

I will tell her about your deep, genuine emphasis on the value of education, and especially of literature; I will tell her about your love of classical music... of taking walks, and certainly of swimming.

And I still sometimes hold on to your shirt, the last Persian Blue cotton shirt you wore on that little boat, your very last hours.

I read your books with your highlighted passages (I love doing that), and then I get sad... your favorite things to highlight are often in the land of the Blues.

I wish you could see Darya and me dancing to the Mississippi Blues.

I remember dancing on your toes to the song "You are my destiny... you are my happiness," which was probably not the most helpful thing in allowing me to work through my Oedipus, but you loved my mother deeply, and I always knew that... and this disturbance, this cruel disturbance, was invaluable in allowing me to move toward oceans of my own.

I have mourned you, instead of cruelly burying you alive every day, in the name of some false libidinal Faithfulness.

I mourned you when I learned how to really love you; in melancholia we hate too much.

We both know that the turbulences of our deeply intimate relationship had that potential lurking around at all times... sometimes I got so close to the timelessness, to the ambivalence, and I still do, but...

Most of the time it is love and gratefulness that I have for you: to have been my father, to have given me your mother's name while allowing me nicknames of my own, for having been Parviz Homayounpour, my father, a father much closer to the image of Jacob Freud than to your own father. You were in search of adult literacy programs all your life, all over the world, and I founded a psychoanalytic group in the name of a literacy of my own, the Freudian Group of Tehran, in the name of transmitting psychoanalytic knowledge, an amalgamation of our desires, mine and yours... ours.

I keep listening to the Blues—not thinking of you alone on that boat right before your heart gave up, but of you being so capable of pleasure that you went for a swim every day, always with your favorite Swiss chocolate, and the way you went across that lake was novelesque—indeed, like the ending of a Kundera novel... you would like this ending... you would romanticize it, and I would get frustrated by your romanticization of the very scene that took you away from me.

Your last view before you jumped into Lake Leman that August 23 must have very much looked like this postcard Kundera had sent you years back, one that I found on your desk near the framed pictures of all your loved ones.

Figure 1 Postcard from Kundera to my father

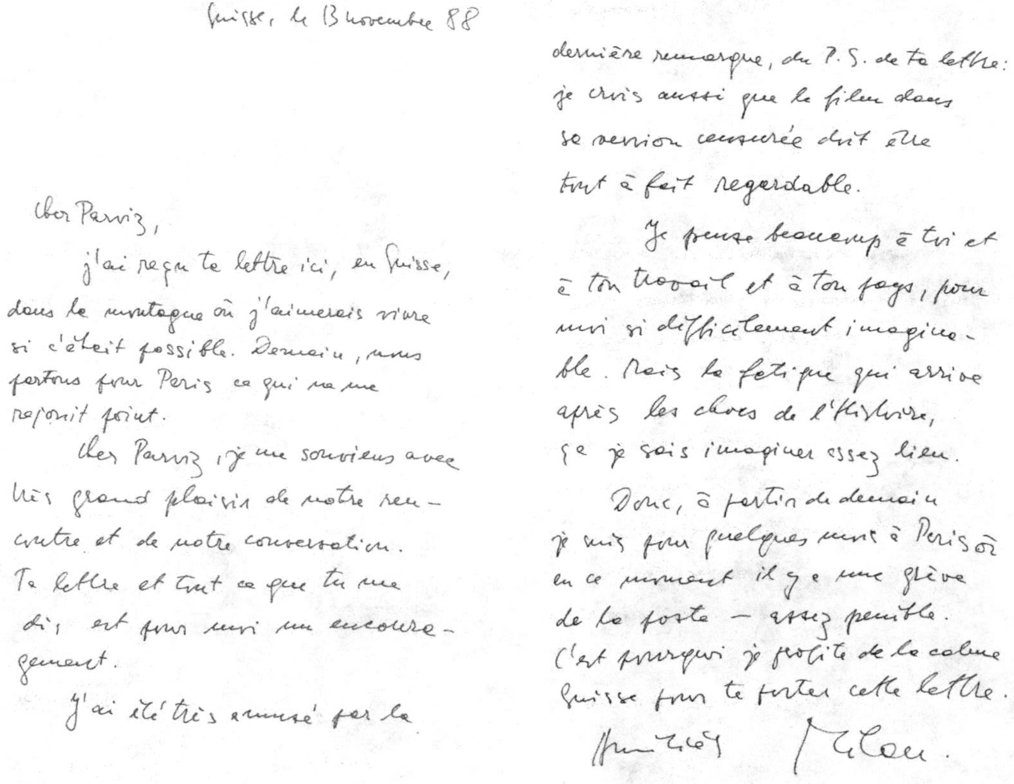

Suisse, le 13 novembre 88

Cher Parviz,

J'ai reçu ta lettre ici, en Suisse, dans le montagne où j'aimerais vivre si c'était possible. Demain, nous partons pour Paris ce qui ne me réjouit point.

Cher Parviz, j'ai un souvenirs avec très grand plaisir de notre rencontre et de notre conversation. Ta lettre et tout ce que tu nous dis est pour moi une émouvantement.

J'ai été très touché par la dernière remarque, ou P.S. de ta lettre: je suis aussi que le film dans ce dernier exprimé était elle tout à fait regardable.

Je pense beaucoup à toi et à ton travail et à ton pays, pour moi si difficilement imaginable. Hélas, mais le peu que j'ai appris après les choses de l'Histoire, ce je sais imaginer assez bien.

Donc, à partir de demain je suis pour quelques jours à Paris où en ce moment il y a une grève de la poste — assez pénible. (C'est pourquoi je profite de la calme Suisse pour te poster cette lettre.)

Mon cher,
Kundera.

Figure 2 Letter from Kundera to my father (November 1988)

In your diaries I also found this letter that Kundera had written to you, a great many notes that you had written on him, on your meetings with him and other correspondence that you had with him, but some things must remain a secret.

My mourning has never been silent, it has always hummed to the tunes of the Blues... my mourning has not been silent, for you gave me language, the ability to go beyond. For no matter how distorted things got, the portrait remained clear; this is what Kundera beautifully elaborates on Francis Bacon's portraits:

> Looking at Bacon's portraits, I am amazed that, despite their "distortion," they all look like their subject. But how can an image look like a subject of which it is consciously, programmatically, a distortion? And yet it does look like the subject; photos of the persons portrayed bear that out; and even if I did not know those photos, it is clear that in all the triptychs, the various deformations of the face resemble one another, so that one recognizes in them some one and same person. However "distorted," these portraits are faithful. That is what I find miraculous.[1]

Then I dreamt of Anahita, the goddess of water, another granddaughter of yours, who is the quintessential divinity of water. When you disappeared that day in the cruel/cold waters while swimming, you were working on your next project, entitled the "Anahita Collection."

Do you remember that midsummer day when you took my brother and me on that little fishing boat on the Caspian Sea, to teach us how to swim? You were holding me horizontally, using both your hands to support me, teaching me how to move my hands and feet, and at one point suddenly you let me go,

Figure 3 Letter from Kundera to my father

you just let me swim on my own. I got scared at first, and turned back to look at you, and in your gaze I saw that you "believed," and you said: "Go on, you are swimming, enjoy..."

I will never forget the exhilarating feeling of the opening up of the possibilities of a "beyond" to our little pond into the big ocean, which you inaugurated for me that day. I think it had to do with a combination of your believing gaze and your timing. Too soon would have been traumatic, and too late would have communicated a lack of faith in my capacities for the beyond. That day, you let go of your eggplant stew dreams forever, in order for me to explore Oceans far, far away. For we can only reach beyond melancholia, away from the proximity and familiarity of our ponds, discovering oceans in Calibanesque geographies, if we learn how to swim via a believing gaze at the right time. Otherwise we are in danger of drowning in a wished-for oceanic feeling.

The night before I finished this book, I had a dream that I was limping... leaving aside the blatantly obvious and various psychoanalytic interpretations of the dream, and taking a clue, as I always do, from the "timing" and the free associations, well, it was the night before the end of this book, and as soon as I woke up, I thought of the words of the poet (the last lines of "Die Beiden Gulden," a version by Rückert of one of the Maqamat al-Hariri), which Freud quotes at the end of *Beyond the Pleasure Principle*: "What we cannot reach flying, we must reach limping, the book tells us it is not a sin to limp."[2]

And I think the dream is a dream that I have dived into the various shades of the Blues, definitely not flying but limping. One can write only if one is willing for the world to see one limping.

The doorbell to my office is ringing, waking me up from this long, elaborate dream. I feel dizzy, as though I am between two worlds, that of the underwater and that of the land. How long have I been dreaming? Has it all been a dream?

The doorbell rings again and again. By the third ring, I am awake enough to open the door.

It's Mrs. N, the protagonist of *Doing Psychoanalysis in Tehran*, my six o'clock patient. She is in Tehran for a visit from Paris, and she has asked to see me. I feel as if I have been out of time and space, telling stories, writing, fantasizing in a wonderland of my own. I open the door to the familiar face of Mrs. N, and right away she says: "Ah, I see some things don't change, Doctor, you look as though you were sleeping right before my session. Did you fall asleep as a defense against seeing me after all these years?" I respond: Some things indeed never change, come in, let us begin.

Notes

1 LV, "Milan Kundera—The Painter's Brutal Gesture: On Francis Bacon."
2 Freud, *Beyond the Pleasure Principle*.

Index

For Product Safety Concerns and Information please contact our EU
representative GPSR@taylorandfrancis.com
Taylor & Francis Verlag GmbH, Kaufingerstraße 24, 80331 München, Germany

www.ingramcontent.com/pod-product-compliance
Lightning Source LLC
Chambersburg PA
CBHW070345270326
41926CB00017B/3998

* 9 7 8 1 0 3 2 2 1 5 9 4 5 *